'This is a well-written account... full of witty observations, a vivid sense of place and wonderful descriptions of people encountered along the way... Hilary and Mollie (the Connemara pony she bought) were strangers... but as they travelled together through Ireland an extraordinary bond grew between them. Their relationship and their journey are described with such honesty and warmth that I began to feel I was riding alongside, experiencing every joy and setback.'

Victoria Eveleigh, author of *A Stallion called Midnight*

'Hilary Bradt recalls her journey across rural Ireland among the people of Galway, Mayo, Clare and Kerry in the 1980s in this sweet — and surreptitiously affecting — memoir... An ode to her youth, horses, Ireland and a momentous event many years ago, *Connemara Mollie* is ultimately a tribute to an unusually personable white pony. The irrepressible Hilary promises a second volume (with a happy ending).'

Longitude, USA

'The straightforward travel diary structure is engaging, but it is the tale of Bradt's relationship with her pony that really sets this traveller's tale apart... A remove of 25 years brings a sense of clarity to the book – she is able to relate with a reflective, dispassionate tone. Her writing is never showy, but she has an ability to capture people and places in a few short sentences. This true-life adventure has a charm all of its own.'

The Connemara Journal

'The writer has an unfailing honesty and self deprecating humour that make you glad that although she made the journey on her own, she is still willing to share it with you... This is the story of a brave Connemara pony, and her rider, the relationship between the two of them described with an obvious, but understated, love. It continues in another volume, *Dingle Peggy*. I will be queuing up to get a copy.'

Books and M...

About the Author

Hilary Bradt grew up in the Chilterns and trained as an occupational therapist, a profession she pursued in the USA and South Africa to finance her ever-longer periods of travel. Eventually the travel bug took over completely, and with her husband George she spent four years backpacking through South America and Africa, founding Bradt Enterprises (now Bradt Travel Guides) along the way. She returned to England to concentrate on writing and publishing, punctuated by summers working as a tour leader. Her books include *Slow Devon and Exmoor*, ten editions of the *Bradt guide to Madagascar* and *Connemara Mollie*, the first part of her Irish journey on horseback. Hilary now lives in semi-retirement in Devon, dividing her time between writing, sculpting and pottering around the county (http://hilarybradt.com).

She was awarded an MBE in 2008.

Dingle Peggy

Further travels in Ireland on horseback

by **Hilary Bradt**

Bradt

First published in the UK in July 2013 by

Bradt Travel Guides Ltd
IDC House, The Vale, Chalfont St Peter, Bucks SL9 9RZ, England
www.bradtguides.com

Print edition published in the USA by The Globe Pequot Press Inc,
PO Box 480, Guilford, Connecticut 06437-0480

Text copyright © 2013 Hilary Bradt
Photographs copyright © 2013 Hilary Bradt
Illustrations copyright © 2013 Hilary Bradt
Map copyright © 2013 Bradt Travel Guides Ltd, drawn by David McCutcheon FBCart.S
Edited by Shelagh Boyd
Proofread by Janet Mears
Typesetting from the author's files by Artinfusion
Cover design: illustration and concept by Neil Gower,
            typesetting by Creative Design and Print

ISBN: 978 1 84162 480 8 (print)
e-ISBN: 978 1 84162 770 0 (e-pub)
e-ISBN: 978 1 84162 672 7 (mobi)

British Library Cataloguing in Publication Data
A catalogue record for this book is available from the British Library

Print production managed by Jellyfish Print Solutions; printed in India
Digital conversion by Scott Gibson

To Harry Ponsonby, whose stories about Irish life
are scattered throughout this book.

With love and thanks.

Prologue

The journey so far: Mollie's story

It was something I'd always wanted to do. Inspired by a pony book when I was 12 or so, I'd spent my youth planning a long-distance horse ride, finally achieving it in 1984 when I bought Mollie from Willy Leahy in Loughrea, Co Galway. Mollie was my dream pony, the pony we could never afford when I was a child. She was a 14.2 hands light-grey Connemara mare; strong, clever, reliable and my increasingly trusting and trusted companion.

During the previous couple of years I had assembled the kit necessary to be self-sufficient with one pony, purchasing a head collar in Peru, expedition saddlebags and a hobble from America, an ex-Indian army saddle in Bucks and making, buying or scrounging the rest of the tack locally. I travelled with a small tent, sleeping bag and Camping Gaz cooking stove and followed no set route. My aim was solely to see the most beautiful parts of Ireland and to fulfil this lifelong dream of not having to turn for home at the end of each day on horseback.

Mollie and I travelled together for a month, covering around 450 miles from her home in Galway, up into Mayo, then south through Clare and into Kerry. It was during my attempt to cross the mountains of the Dingle Peninsula that Mollie met her death. This story is told in *Connemara Mollie*.

I stubbornly hung on to that dream, however. It had been too long in the planning, too persistent in my imagination to let go. So although I returned to England for six weeks, I knew I would come back to Ireland. If I abandoned the ride now I would only look back on the adventure with sadness and – more importantly – I would never again feel the carefree enjoyment of off-road riding. I had not only lost my way on the Dingle Peninsula, I had lost my confidence.

I left my luggage with the Hennessy family who took me in after Mollie's death, and asked them to look out for a replacement pony. I told them I would return in July, and I kept my word.

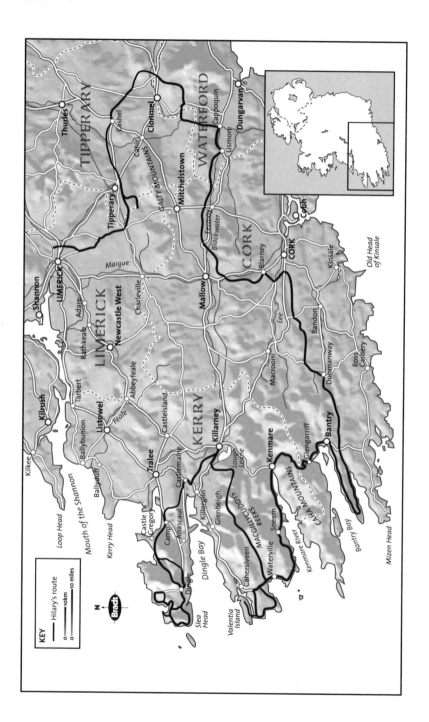

Chapter 1

"That's the house!" I said, relieved at recognising it after a gap of six weeks. It was the second good omen of the day, the first being the ease with which I'd hitched a lift to Castle Gregory from Tralee. I carried little luggage; most of the necessities for the next stage of my journey were stored at the Hennessys. Except a horse. And my courage.

A small white pony was grazing in the adjacent paddock and my heart quickened. Was it for me? But it wasn't even a pony. Looking more closely I saw long ears. Then Noel emerged from the house and I was immediately enfolded into the warmth of the family. Noel's mum, Kathleen, put the kettle on and showed me into the spare bedroom. My luggage was in the shed, a bit cobwebby, but intact. There was Mollie's precious saddle, and the saddlebags, and all the bits and pieces I needed to continue my trek. Memories flooded back and I resolutely chased them away. Now was the time to look forward.

As soon as I dared, I raised the subject of a replacement horse or pony. Had someone heard about Mollie's death and offered me a mount? No, but Pedar would fix me up with something for sure. He was the local horse dealer and, incidentally, the owner of the animal in the field. It was a jennet (donkey mother, pony father) and was in disgrace. Pedar had sold it to a local man to pull a cart, but the animal was frightened by the white lines on the road (I can understand that; in 1984 they were a rarity) and had bolted. Before Pedar took it back, Noel was planning to use it for farm work but it was more interested in chasing sheep than helping to round them up, so had to be hobbled. He was a sturdy-looking animal so I asked if I could try riding him; I rather fancied travelling around Ireland on a jennet. But his appearance was deceptive. He turned out to be shaped like one of those toys you make out of a Styrofoam ball and matchsticks. There was nowhere to put the saddle on the spherical body, and when I mounted bareback I nearly fell off the other side.

I didn't want to impose on the Hennessy family any longer than necessary, so it was a matter of urgency to find a suitable mount. In those days few country people had a phone, so arranging to meet Pedar was a complicated process. First, one of the boys drove me to his house in Dingle, only to find that he wasn't in. But everyone is related here so his wife knew all about me. Her sister runs the B&B in Anascaul where I stayed the last night before my fateful ride over the mountains with Mollie. We arranged for Pedar to phone us at a nearby – nearish-by – hotel. This constituted a Night Out for Kathleen, who was dressed up to the nines including some rather startling purple shoes. When she opened the van she let out a wail. "Oh Jesus God, can you believe this?" Noel had used it to transport sheep, and the back of the vehicle bore evidence that they had enjoyed plenty of food and drink before setting out. "Oh Jesus, oh Sacred Heart, I'm telling you, girlie, I *scrubbed* that van out only last week, oh dear God…" At the hotel she made a beeline for the slot machine, and a few minutes later Pedar left a message that he'd be over next morning. Guinness and conversation flowed, Kathleen was eventually prised away from her gambling, and someone took us home in a cleaner vehicle.

Next morning, Sunday, I accompanied the family to Mass although my spiritual sustenance was limited to a walk in the misty sunshine to look for a phone box. I wanted to give my parents a progress report. The telephone operator's Sunday was clearly transformed by this break from the routine business of listening in to local calls. At first there was no reply, but he said, "Sure but I'll try again to show there's no hard feelings." When my sleepy-sounding mother finally answered, he let me chat for at least ten minutes – I'd paid for three – so the conversation must have been absorbing. Telecom operators in those days wielded considerable power. I was told a story about a businessman whose patience snapped at the telephonist's leisurely approach to her job and swore at her down the phone. It was probably a regular occurrence but this time he went too far and the operator cut him off. Not for a few minutes but for two months. His wife and daughter were able to make calls, but not him. Even when he tried to phone from friends' houses the operator's ever-listening ear discovered the deception and she unplugged him. Exactly two months after his oaths, he was re-instated.

When we got back to the house, there was Pedar banging some shoes onto a nondescript brown pony with a silly hairstyle. I looked at it in dismay. "It's awfully small!" I said doubtfully.

"She's perfect." (bang bang) "Carry you all day. Never gets tired." The pony couldn't have been more than 13.2 hands and I'm no midget.

"Don't you have anything else? Something bigger?" He shook his head. "What's her name?"

"Peggy. Pure Connemara," he added as an afterthought.

So I saddled up and trotted up and down the road and cantered in the field.

"She's got very low head carriage," I said snootily. This was putting it mildly; her neck was never above the horizontal.

Pedar stared at me. "D'you want a show pony or a worker? She'll do you fine. I drive her all day in my gig." Which explained the muscular neck, partially cropped mane to accommodate the collar, and brisk trot.

I really didn't like this pony. She was too small, too plain, and I couldn't forgive her for not being Mollie. But it didn't look as though I'd find anything else. Not for hire, anyway. We all went into the kitchen for cups of tea and business talk, but it was soon obvious that what Pedar thought was a fair rental fee and what I could afford to pay were very different. We argued back and forth for ages and failed to come to an agreement, so I suggested that I'd ride her the 13 miles to Dingle next day with the saddlebags, see if she was suitable, and we could discuss it further then.

After lunch I sat in the paddock and watched Peggy grazing, willing myself to like her. She had a thick neck, a sausage-shaped body and working-class tufts of hair on her fetlocks. Certainly no show pony. But perhaps I'd been unfair to call her a nondescript brown; she was actually the colour of a freshly-pulled pint of Guinness, with touches of foamy beige including a mealy muzzle like an Exmoor pony, and blonde streaks in her mane. But after Mollie, who drew admiring glances from everyone, Peggy was a definite comedown. I decided to go on a longer ride that afternoon, before encumbering her with saddlebags, so took a grassy track towards the mountains. When she felt soft turf beneath her hooves, instead of tarmac, Peggy stopped dead in surprise. Oh brave new world! Without her accustomed blinkers she could see mountains and sky – except that if she wanted to look at something above her she tilted her head sideways to peep under the imaginary blinkers while keeping her neck resolutely horizontal. It was very endearing and made me laugh out loud. Her brown ears were so sharply pricked that they almost met in the middle, and I was happy to enjoy her nice fast walk without trying anything more ambitious. Perhaps she wasn't so bad.

ʊ   ʊ   ʊ

My evening with the Hennessys was everything I love about Ireland, full of laughter and conviviality. When I stayed there after Mollie's death I was too numbed by grief to appreciate the family properly. Kathleen was my favourite, not just for her turn of phrase and stories, but for what she had achieved. Having been brought up in a remote stone cottage at the foot of the cliffs in the Valley of the Cows, she had raised eight children, all of whom were doing well, some spectacularly so. She told me that two were in New York, one working as a Vogue fashion model, and that a daughter was in charge of customer relations in a posh hotel in the United Arab Emirates. Yet Sylvester, the oldest boy, said he remembered going barefoot to the village school where all ages were taught together in the one-room schoolhouse. Kathleen had visited the New York son and daughter, but didn't feel she could go again, despite their entreaties and promise of an air ticket because, "Imagine the state of the house when I get back. Those two boys would burn the bottoms out of all the pans! Oh Lord, I couldn't risk it."

While the family chatted, I worked with needle and thread, mending the saddlebags and adapting the tack to Peggy's diminutive size. I shortened the girth and the belly strap that kept the saddlebags in place, and checked that the little straps that I'd used to attach Mollie's snaffle bit to the head collar were undamaged. Her splendid Peruvian head collar had been lost, so I had bought a strong nylon one in England. Not as glamorous as Mollie's but virtually indestructible.

Peggy still managed to get rid of it during the night. I'd left the head collar on to avoid a repeat of my early experience with Mollie when she wanted as little to do with me as possible and I'd spent two hours trying to catch her. However, a family search found the head collar trampled into the grass and Peggy was cooperative. She submitted to all the pushing and shoving and tightening of girths and straps that loading the saddlebags entailed, and when I led her round experimentally she didn't seem bothered by all the extra encumbrance. Probably not much different from her accustomed harness. And it was certainly less effort to load a smaller pony – heaving the bags onto

Mollie's back used to take all my strength. The size advantage was reinforced when I mounted. Much easier.

ᘔ ᘔ ᘔ

My route to Dingle was unadventurous. I had no intention of trying a cross-country route, even though the map showed some possibilities. Indeed, I wondered if I would ever feel brave enough to leave the tarmac again. Mollie's death in the trackless, boggy interior had given my confidence a severe shaking. Yesterday, during my ride along that track towards those fateful mountains, fear had bubbled up inside me. To be responsible for the health and safety of a trusting animal is such a big thing. Peggy had her own issues with cross-country work, so set off happily in the direction of Dingle and home. This was when I realised that she was in season. She neighed seductively at every horse we passed, and hopefully into empty landscape when there was no equine in sight.

The road to Dingle was as scenic as I could have wished for. Peggy walked cheerfully past the bulk of Stradbally Mountain, and up the hill towards Conor Pass, Ireland's highest motorable road. Not that there were many motors on it that day. The narrow lane is cut into the hillside, and the challenges facing the drivers were evident in their tense expressions as they inched past me. For my part, it was wonderful. I just sat there admiring the scenery, while Peggy did all the work. The craggy, rock-strewn mountains harboured little lakes in their valleys and wisps of cloud on the peaks. Shaggy black-faced sheep grazed on the coarse grass and hooded crows circled above. At the top of the pass I dismounted to let Peggy get her breath back and graze while I ate the picnic lunch that Kathleen had provided. A local man came over to admire Peggy. "That's Pedar's pony isn't it?" I explained about my ride – and Mollie – and he wished me luck.

I knew where I was headed in Dingle. The youth hostel had a campsite and a paddock for Peggy. My tiny tent was dwarfed by the nearby luxury canvas houses and it seemed strange to have a toilet/shower block at my disposal. With Mollie I had usually found a river to wash in or brought water to heat in the tent. Then, nervously, I went to see Pedar. I knew I wanted to hire Peggy; he was right, she was fine for the job. We just had to settle on a price that I could afford. Pedar was expecting me – he had just got back from helping the Hennessy boys with some sheep dipping – and said he needed a pint of Guinness before we could talk. But of course, once in the pub, I realised that we couldn't talk business without the other customers hanging on every word, so I chatted to them about my plans. "Ah yes," said one of them, "I saw a person yesterday riding through town on a horse all covered in luggage. But t'was a man." No it wasn't, it was me. I remembered the stares as I self-consciously rode past the shops. Glancing in the reflecting windows I could see a mound of beige-coloured luggage topped by a blue, shapeless lump with a little brown head sticking out of one end, a tail out of the other, and a set of twinkling legs underneath. I decided, now the weather was getting warmer, I'd better wear my tightest T-shirt. When we'd all finished our drinks I told Pedar I'd come to his house the next day to conclude our discussion.

Back in the tent, with the cheery sound of happy campers all around me, I sank into despondency. I was mourning the loss of Mollie both as my best equine friend and the most expensive item I'd ever bought. Could Peggy ever replace her in my affections and how was I going to afford to hire her anyway? Having set out on the Mollie trek with only very vague plans, I now had a rough route in mind, and the idea that my target should be a thousand miles in total. I would feel I had achieved something then. I'd worked out that Mollie and I had done about 450 miles in a month, but the first week was spent on an organised trek without luggage so we covered more ground;

I reckoned I'd need to hire Peggy for at least six weeks, so Pedar's weekly fee was looking prohibitive.

Next day was my birthday, and it didn't start well. At 2am a group of French arrived from the pub in high spirits and settled into the tent next to mine with much shouting and laughing. I got so fed up I yelled at them to be quiet. It worked for only a few minutes.

Tired and still cross in the morning, I went back to Pedar's house and, with no-one listening to the conversation, came to an agreement quite quickly. Rather than a weekly charge he agreed that I could keep Peggy as long as I wanted – within reason. What a relief! "And you don't have to bring her back to Dingle. Leave her with Ted O'Connell near Limerick and I'll pick her up."

So I packed up the tent and went to give Peggy the 2lbs of carrots I'd generously bought her as a birthday present (someone might as well receive a present today). I found her standing outside the paddock near the collapsed gate. She took one look at me and my carrots and galloped off across someone's immaculate lawn. When I approached she trotted off again, taking a short cut across the porch steps where she very nearly fell, before being headed off and caught by the hostel warden, a pleasant young Australian who was accustomed to horses. Poor Peggy, she thought she'd come home to her boyfriend and familiar surroundings. No wonder she didn't want to have anything to do with me. I led her self-consciously to the campsite and took an age to get all the gear in place, watched by a growing crowd of campers. I gave pony rides to a couple of kids, then mounted with a flourish – and fell off the other side in front of the odious French group.

I headed west out of Dingle, down a lane sheltered by high hedges sculpted by the wind and past gardens boastfully sporting palm trees, to Ventry Strand. I wanted to give Peggy her first beach experience. The narrow, mauvish-coloured stretch of sand is backed by grass-covered dunes and cut by a stream. Walkers cross by the little footbridge but I wanted to test Peggy's competence at fording rivers. Mollie used to take this request in her stride, even quite deep rivers. But she had no fear of water, and regularly swam in the sea. Peggy's experience was quite different. She stopped, wide-eyed in astonishment at the edge of the beach, with much snorting, and it took quite a while to persuade her that it was safe to set hoof on it. She tiptoed warily along the firm sand (it was low tide) as though crossing a minefield, shying at the menacing lumps of seaweed. My suggestion that she approach the surf was too much for any sensible pony – here was water advancing at a gallop. No wonder she fled! Gradually her snorting became more subdued, and by the time we'd reached the river she'd managed a rather wobbly canter, I'd just avoided falling off, and she'd paddled in an un-wavy bit of shallow water. But she had no intention of wading across the river. Considering it was the first time she'd been to the seaside (despite living in a seaside town), I told her she'd been very brave and allowed her to return the way we'd come.

ひ ひ ひ

I was heading for Slea Head on the westernmost part of the Dingle Peninsula. The road wraps itself around Mount Eagle, hugging the rocky coast where slanting grey shards of rock pierce the sky. Perilous waters, these. An old shipwreck still lay half-submerged by the cliff, a reminder that two ships from the Spanish Armada met their end here in 1588: the *Santa Maria de la Rosa* and the *San Juan*. Slea Head has always been one of Dingle's main tourist attractions so even in 1984 there were plenty of cars sharing the route with me. A sign advertising 'Beehive Huts' caught my eye and, having read about these stone structures, I decided to dismount and take a look. The Irish name is *clochán*, but 'beehive' perfectly describes their shape: squat little domes of roughly shaped stone, corbelled at the top so they needed no mortar. They could date from the 12th century, so I was told, and may have been dwellings although they seemed better suited to the hens that were living there. When I got back to Peggy, an elderly woman and her grandchildren were staring at all the luggage. I explained what I was doing. She found the idea that one could ride around Ireland almost impossible to comprehend. "But where do you sleep? Dear Lord, do you? Outside? Oh Jesus! What do you eat? Oh dear God…"

A track led tantalisingly to the most westerly mainland point in Europe, Dunmore Head, but it looked boggy and I was too nervous to try it. Instead I clip-clopped my way toward Dunquin, where the cliff rises sheer and black above the road and the local houses are built from the same dark stone. By the evening the clouds had cleared and the low sun lit the cliffs and turned the sea from grey to turquoise. I'd been keeping Great Blasket Island in sight but now the hazy silhouettes of other islands came into view, the perfect pyramids of Tearaght and the endearing profile of The Sleeping Giant, his hand resting on his pot belly and his mouth open above his crinkly beard.

At Dunquin I asked directions to the youth hostel. Yes, they had a bed but the warden didn't know where I could put Peggy. I'd spotted a likely-looking field next door, so went to ask at the adjacent house. A young boy answered my knock and I heard him go to the next room and relay my question in a language I didn't recognise. I was invited through to where a large family was eating dinner. In one fluid movement his mother had cleared a place, pulled up a chair, poured some tea and plonked two sausages on a plate. I felt quite dazed as I munched and slurped. "Didn't you know that Dingle is a Gaeltacht region?"

Eileen explained what that meant: Irish is spoken in the home in many households and the government provides a subsidy to encourage its use. Only the two boys were hers; there was a niece over from America and two girls –

cousins – here from Cork to perfect their Irish. The whole room glowed with family warmth and goodwill. My English inhibitions melted and I heard myself say that it was my birthday. They all sang 'Happy Birthday' in Irish and added the greeting 'May you live to be 100'. My birthday was turning out very well indeed. Reluctantly, I said I must go since Peggy was tied up outside the hostel (had I known then that this was the last time I could safely leave her tied, I might have stayed longer). Father said she could go in the big field and Patrick, the young boy, took me there. When I saw it was huge and full of good grass I decided to stay two nights and visit Great Blasket Island which lay four miles off Slea Head.

This was a good decision. Great Blasket is gorgeous and just right for a day's walking. Until 1953 when the whole island was evacuated, there used to be a population of hardy fisherfolk, all of whom seem to have written books which have become classics in the Irish language. No, that's an exaggeration, but the three best-known ones have been translated into English: *An Old Woman's Reflections* by Peig Sayers, *Twenty Years A-Growing* by Maurice O'Sullivan (or Muiris Ó Súilleabháin if you prefer) and *The Islandman* by Tomás Ó Criomhthain. O'Sullivan's title comes from the traditional division of man's fourscore years: twenty a-growing, twenty a-blossoming, twenty a-stooping and twenty declining.

A sea mist all but obscured the island when I boarded the ferry, and on arrival the other passengers made a beeline for the café. I headed up the rough path to the northern end, climbing steadily in the mist and uneasily aware of a silhouetted figure keeping his distance behind me. At the highest point, just under a thousand feet high, the sun broke through the mist and gradually revealed the glorious view. With the aid of my map I could identify Valentia Island to the south, across Dingle Bay, and the blue mountain range of MacGillycuddy's Reeks to the east. I hoped to reach both places within the next couple of weeks.

The stalker turned out to be a pleasant German who was planning to camp on the island, and we ate a companionable chocolate bar together before I headed briskly back to catch the ferry. Numerous rabbits were sunning themselves outside their burrows, and I identified a lone curlew and oystercatchers on the shore. Green headlands speckled with white sheep were broken by scooped-out sandy bays. Too bad there was not enough time for a swim.

Back in the youth hostel, after checking on Peggy, I wrote this limerick in the youth hostel guestbook:

From England to Ireland, I travelled by ferry
And rode on a pony from Galway to Kerry.
Asked a lady from Arkansas
"Say, aren't you saddle-sore?"
And the pony and I both said "Very!"

Peggy had had a good rest and was eager to get going, though our planned destinations differed. She was still hoping to go home, whereas my route continued round Slea Head to Ballyferriter. I had bought some spray-on insect repellent in Dingle and with the warm, still weather bringing out a mass of flies, I wanted to protect her face from this irritation. After loading her up, I tied her to the fence post and, cupping my hand over her eye to protect it, I let out a jet of spray. I don't know what it was that frightened her so much – the noise of the aerosol, or some previous bad experience? – but she pulled back with such force that the concrete post broke. Concrete! She was unbelievably strong. Fortunately the new head collar I'd bought in England proved itself almost indestructible. Later, I needed to tie her up again while I bought provisions from a village shop, but this time I tied her to a telegraph pole. Horses never forget; now that being tied was linked in her mind with danger, she once again pulled back with all her strength. I could see her muscles bulging with the effort. This time nothing broke, so I hoped she would think twice about doing it again.

Soon after we'd set out, Peggy was thrilled to see two horses ahead of her. We caught them up and I was less thrilled when the man accompanying them asked if I was going to Ballyferriter and when I said yes, he said, "Good, I'm tired, they can go with you," and turned them loose on the road. I refused to go along with his plan. The thought of being in charge of two loose horses on a busy narrow road for four miles and then waiting around in town with them for a tired (and no doubt thirsty) farmer, didn't appeal to me. He exploded into a stream of curses. "Go on, trot up the road!" he commanded. I walked and the loose horses investigated someone's drive. More oaths. So I trotted and they trotted behind until I slowed near a track leading into the mountains. Obviously familiar territory to the horses, which cantered away with the farmer, still cursing, at the rear. I was very relieved to see them go. Peggy, however, never got over her disappointment. She neighed hopefully every five minutes or so throughout the day, and scanned the countryside for her new friends. Poor Peggy. I had taken her away from her home and companions, and I was learning that she was the most sociable pony I'd ever met. If she were a person she would have been a party-going extrovert and a chatterbox. Depriving her of equine company made me feel permanently guilty.

U　U　U

My goal that day was the Gallarus Oratory, an early Christian chapel reputed to be the most interesting tourist site in Dingle. I asked directions from a fellow tidying the graveyard in the local church.

"Well, you see that – er – d'ye see it? In the valley?"

"See what?"

"Well do you see it?"

I tried to follow his directions but went the wrong way, heading for the wrong 'it'. When I finally got there I had to agree that Gallarus was, indeed, remarkable. Often described as being the shape of an inverted boat, it is constructed on a rectangular base from individually cut stones, carefully laid to create inward-curving walls which meet at the top. A doorway facing due west gives entrance to its dry interior, and it was not hard to imagine services taking place here all those years ago. Estimates vary as to when it was built, but it was somewhere between the 8th and 12th century. It has never been restored and is still watertight. The corbelled roof reminded me of Mayan architecture, so maybe St Brendan did get to the Americas as is often speculated. I paid only a quick visit since I was preoccupied with the vision of Peggy galloping away, towing a gate behind her, and as a reward for her staying tied I led her down the road feeling that a bottom/back rest would do us both good. Several cars passed, the occupants staring more than usual. Eventually I glanced round and saw that Peggy was walking briskly along with pricked ears, while her saddle and luggage dangled beneath her belly. Mollie used to stop when that happened, but Peggy seems to accept it as part of the day's measure of discomfort. Everything had to be taken off in the road, while queues of cars on their way to the Oratory waited for me to finish.

I dropped down to the coast, passed through the village of Ballydavid, and got permission from a farmer to camp in his field. It was a beautiful spot, with plenty of grass for Peggy and for me a view over Smerwick harbour to Dún an Óir. This was the scene of one of England's most shameful episodes in its seemingly endless attempts to subdue the Irish. In the 16th century, Henry VIII decided it was time to establish control of Ireland, which had deteriorated, in the monarch's eyes, to a country of chieftains who 'maketh war and peace for himself without any licence of the King'. His scheme of 'surrender and regrant', whereby chiefs surrendered their land to the Crown but received it back if they agreed to be ruled by English law, was not well received, especially since conversion to Protestantism was part of the deal. The Irish rebelled. When Elizabeth came to the throne she was determined to finish the job and sent her Lord Deputy of Ireland, General Arthur Grey, to deal with the rebels. These were not all Irish. In 1580 Pope Gregory XIII financed an invading force of 600 Italian, Spanish and Basque men who sailed into Smerwick harbour to come to the aid of the Irish rebels, of whom only 17 managed to join them on the tip of the Dingle Peninsula. The geography of the place made Lord Grey's job relatively easy, and his men laid siege to Dún an Óir, attacking from both the sea and land.

The 'Papists' were hopelessly outnumbered and outweaponed, and had to contend not only with Grey's 4,000 soldiers but his thirst for revenge: he'd earlier lost 800 troops in an unsuccessful battle in Co Wicklow. Inevitably the Catholics eventually surrendered. Had they known what was to happen to them, they would have fought on. When the three Irish leaders, including a priest, refused to accept the religious supremacy of the Queen, Grey ordered his blacksmith to break the bones in their hands and feet and, for good measure, to cut off the priest's finger and thumb which had touched the Sacrament of the Eucharist. They were hanged 24 hours later. After formally surrendering their weapons and ensigns, the foreigners were all put to death.

I knew none of this bloody history as I sat outside the tent writing my diary and watching the sun slide below the headland. Peggy, meanwhile, was staring longingly through the bars of the gate, looking like an Amnesty International poster. She wanted to go home.

υ   υ   υ

My circuit of the Dingle Peninsula was almost complete. I had achieved my purpose of doing some gentle sightseeing while getting used to Peggy and – more importantly – she to me. She learned faster than I did, conveying her needs and wishes as eloquently as a pony can. I was just very slow on the uptake. One day, instead of her usual brisk walk she dawdled along with her nose to the ground, smelling the tarmac and every now and then stopping to scrape it with her hoof. I couldn't think what was the matter and got quite cross with her. Then she spied a woman crossing her front garden carrying a bucket of water. Peggy raised her head and gave a little whinny. Of course! "Would you mind giving my pony a drink?" I asked. The woman obligingly fetched a fresh bucket of cold water, and Peggy drank gratefully. She taught me always to give her a decent lunch break, too. If I neglected her needs by selfishly tying her up outside a pub, she would trail along afterwards with her head even lower than usual, stopping pointedly when in the vicinity of green grass. She knew better than to try to graze without permission; it was one thing I was strict about.

I had one last bit of sightseeing to achieve before returning to the Dingle youth hostel. Plonked in the northern end of the peninsula is Brandon Mountain, at 3,127 feet the highest peak on Dingle. Indeed, if it were not for MacGillycuddy's Reeks it would be the highest in Ireland, and I had read about the old Saint's Road up to St Brendan's Oratory, the ruins of a beehive-shaped chapel on the summit. It would be a lovely ride and the weather was clear. I had a great affection for St Brendan the Navigator who exemplified serendipitous travel. Having spent a busy time as a priest in the 6th century founding monasteries, he arrived in western Kerry to prepare for his great voyage into the unknown. It is said that he had a vision of the Promised Land while meditating on the mountain named after him. He built a coracle from wattle and hide, filled it with monks, and set forth from Brandon Bay. The voyage lasted seven years. He and his fellow passengers met psalm-singing birds, sea monsters a-plenty, a hermit clad only in hair who had survived for 60 years being fed by an otter, and even encountered a very cold and wet Judas Iscariot sitting on a rock in the ocean on day-release from Hell. He may also have reached America.

When I got to the trail, however, my nerve gave out – I just didn't dare leave the road. I knew I had to get my confidence back, and fortuitously I had a solution. My German friend, Susanne, was arriving in Dingle in a couple of days and would travel with me for a fortnight. It's always easier to be brave in company.

Chapter 2

Knowing my anxious-mother state I should never have offered to loan Peggy. Over breakfast I had struck up a conversation with a pretty young Swedish girl who had asked about my trip and expressed the right amount of admiration and sympathy over Mollie. She owned her own horse in Sweden, she said, and had been trying to hire ponies to go out unaccompanied, but no trekking stable would permit it. "You can take Peggy if you like," I heard myself saying. "I'm having a rest day tomorrow and it'll do her good to be ridden without the luggage." The girl was thrilled and I felt cosily magnanimous.

Peggy was sharing a large field with several sleek and sour heavy horses which pulled the horse-drawn caravans then popular in the area. I'd always been impressed at the courage both of the company trusting their horses to the care of inexperienced visitors, and by the tourists themselves who often knew almost nothing about horses. I arrived in time to watch a Frenchman retreating backwards towards the gate pursued by an evil-looking chestnut mare. One of Peggy's most endearing characteristics was that she'd walk up to me in the morning with a look of anticipation on her face, so handing the Frenchman Peggy's rope, I walked purposefully towards his horse, took its head collar, gave it some of Peggy's bread and led it to its temporary owner who was suitably impressed and grateful. I smiled a gracious we-horse-owners-know-all smile and Peggy pulled her rope out of my slack smug fingers and trotted off to rejoin her friends.

The Swedish girl, her boyfriend and Peggy left at around 11 o'clock and I set out with my picnic to walk round the cliffs of the chunky peninsula south of Dingle. It was another perfect day; very hot and rather hazy, and I relished the thought of being able to explore without Peggy-anxiety. The grassy path to the lighthouse took me close by the edge of deeply indented cliffs, the fluted brown-grey rocks dropping sheer to a dark-blue sea. Now the nesting season was over, there were fewer seabirds, but herring gulls swirled below me along with the occasional black-backed gull. Ireland must have some of the finest cliff scenery in the world, but even more exciting than the landscape were the dozens of mushrooms I could see glinting in the grass in the nearby meadows. I react to a field of mushrooms as a fox does to a barn full of chickens. The joy of the grab takes over from mere need and I end up with far more than I can possibly eat. The plastic bag I carried back with me contained enough to feed the entire hostel.

Near the entrance to the harbour is a cave known as Nancy Brown's Parlour. It's one of those unexceptional Irish places that become fascinating once you know the legend associated with it. Within the cave, so they say, is a secret passage leading to the house of James Louis Rice who had made his home fit for a queen. His expected guest? Marie Antoinette. Plans were afoot to rescue her from the French Revolution and hide her in Dingle. This extraordinary story becomes plausible when you learn that James Louis's father ran a profitable wine business, his ships regularly plying the ocean between France and Ireland, and that his son was sent to school on the continent. Catholics were deemed unfit for secondary education in British-ruled Ireland. When young James left college he entered the service of the

Emperor of Austria, eventually becoming his close confidante, and joined the Irish Brigade, an exiled band of Irishmen who fought alongside the French. When revolution erupted and the French royal family were imprisoned in Paris, James hatched a plan to use one of the wine ships to spirit Marie Antoinette to Ireland and to safety. They say that it was only the queen's last-minute refusal to leave her family that prevented the success of this course of action. Who Nancy Brown was, no one could tell me.

U   U   U

"No sign of those kids with your pony!" said the warden cheerfully when he saw me. I couldn't believe it; it was nearly 7.30. I looked in my dorm for the saddle but it wasn't there. Nor was Peggy in the field. I was distraught, convinced that something terrible had happened: Peggy had been hit by a car, or had bolted or got caught up in barbed wire. Perhaps the girl or boy had had an accident. Why had I been so stupid as to lend Peggy to a couple I didn't know? She wasn't even my pony to lend! Then, at 8 o'clock, a hosteller on a bicycle reported having seen them about two miles away, and I burst into tears of relief.

Later I felt quite guilty about my anger at the two repentant teenagers. After all, they pointed out, we never agreed that they should go out for only a couple of hours. That was just my assumption.

"But you know what happened to my last pony," I said, my voice trembling. "Couldn't you imagine how worried I'd be?" I managed to introduce a semblance of sincerity into my voice when I said I was glad they'd had a good time.

"And Peggy had a good time too. She loved it!"

I hoped that was true.

U   U   U

The plan to have Susanne join me had been hatched the previous October at Frankfurt Book Fair. Our friendship went back ten years to when Susanne worked on the German translation of the first Bradt guide, and each year we would have dinner together in Frankfurt and catch up on news. In 1983, naturally, I told her excitedly about my plan to do a long-distance ride through Ireland the following year. Susanne looked wistful. "You know what I remember most about my childhood? There was a riding stable nearby, and every minute I went there and cried because we had no money for riding lessons."

"Maybe you could join me for some of the time?"

"But now I'm not so excited about riding. I went with my first boyfriend on a horse and it galloped away and I fell down."

Nevertheless, we were both enthusiastic about doing a trip together so when I bought Mollie in May I wrote to Susanne and described my lovely strong pony who could easily carry extra luggage, and suggested that she join me for a few weeks. We could take it in turns to walk and ride which, at Mollie's slow pace, would not be strenuous. Back in England after Mollie's death I phoned her to discuss the revised plan and agreed that she should come anyway, and if I hadn't found a replacement pony, we'd just have a holiday in Kerry.

Dingle seemed the perfect place to introduce Susanne to Ireland and begin the second part of my journey. A small town with a harbour full of brightly painted boats, green hills beyond and immunity to the effects of tourism, Dingle is the focus for visiting this part of Kerry. 'A troupe of winding streets dancing down a steep slope of rock and gorse' is how my effervescent guidebook described it. I wondered how the locals could remain so friendly when they were in the minority in every pub and shop. Few visitors seemed prepared to risk leaving the main tourist sights, however. During my two-day sortie around the end of the peninsula I'd met only a couple of other foreigners, an Englishman struggling on a bicycle from which panniers and bags hung like clusters of grapes, and an American in a hired car trying to match each stone at Gallarus Oratory to those in his guide book.

Susanne had brought champagne from the Duty Free shop in Shannon. We sat outside with our mushroom soup and mugs full of bubbly and caught up on the news. Afterwards I took her to meet Peggy. "She's got a mouth like my grandmother," she commented.

The following day was another scorcher. Peggy had a well-deserved rest and we went to the beach, had a swim, and collected more mushrooms from the meadows overlooking Dingle harbour. And I speculated about sea monsters living contentedly in the bay, having read an extraordinary 17th-century newspaper report:

> A Wonderful Fish or Beast was lately killed, by James Steward, as it came of its own accord to Him out of the sea to the Shore, where he was alone on Horseback at the Harbour's Mouth of Dingle-Icoush, which had two heads and Ten horns, and upon Eight of the said Horns about 800 buttons or the resemblance of Little Coronets; and in each of them a set of Teeth, the said Body was bigger than a Horse and was 19 Foot Long Horns and all, the great Head thereof Carried only the said ten Horns and two very large Eyes. And the little Head thereof carried a wonderful strange mouth and two Tongues in it.

On first reading, this creature sounds utterly improbable, but then you consider 'about 800 buttons or the resemblance of Little Coronets' on its ten 'horns' and you think, yes, suckers on tentacles – it must have been a giant squid or kraken!

U U U

In the evening Susanne had her first riding lesson. Peggy almost smirked when she realised what was atop her. She'd walk along quietly, a responsible look on her face, butter wouldn't melt in her granny mouth, then as soon as my back was turned she'd plunge her head down to eat, pulling the reins out of Susanne's hands. I had to keep her on a short lead rein. By supper time she was behaving better and Susanne had managed a short trot.

The two of us studied the map and a little booklet describing local walks. "You have to meet the Hennessys, so we need to go over the Conor Pass again, but I'd love to see if we can do it away from the cars." On my first day with Peggy I'd looked longingly at a green road (or boreen) that led southeast from the pass in the direction of Dingle. Now, with two of us, we could try it. Our little walks book showed a route up a minor road which joined this green road. From the description it seemed that there were no locked gates or impassable areas.

Peggy eyed me suspiciously when I went to collect her from the field. Up until now she'd walked towards me with pricked ears. This time she waited for me to come to her. At the hostel I looked properly at Susanne's luggage for the first time. She'd brought a shiny plastic blue-and-white striped duffle bag with a drawstring at one end.

"Why didn't you bring a rucksack?" I asked crossly.

Susanne stared at me. "Because you told me not. You said my luggage must be waterproof, and soft for fixing to the saddle."

Yes, I suppose those had been my instructions but I hadn't thought it through. How was I to attach this bag when there was hardly an inch of Peggy showing under the existing load? The duffle looked more like a laundry bag to me and needed an attachment at each end if I was to fasten it properly to the saddle. We didn't even have any cord with us. I fixed it to the rest of the luggage as best I could, and with Susanne walking beside me, we left Dingle, still bathed in hot sunshine, and headed for the mountains.

The little lane was bordered by flowering fuchsia hedges, their red-and-purple bells trembling above our heads, and led gently uphill toward the gap in the mountains.

Towards the end of the morning we crossed the Garfinny River, stopping to admire Ireland's oldest surviving bridge. This is thought to date from medieval times, and is beautifully constructed without mortar, using the weight of the stones themselves to retain the arch. Lord Grey may have taken his troops across this bridge on his way to Smerwick Harbour, according to a recently erected sign.

Shortly thereafter we turned west to meet our green road. It climbed up sharply, giving us a marvellous view across Dingle Bay to the hazy mountains of the Iveragh Peninsula. As we ate our picnic lunch in a sheltered sunny spot I was full of warm feelings of companionship. I like travelling alone but it was awfully good to be with a friend while I was still getting my courage back.

The track continued half-heartedly then petered out on a bleak hilltop. I could see where we were supposed to go; the Conor Pass car park was clearly visible, as was the grassy green road that had tempted me a week ago, but it was on the other side of a small river valley. 'Judge when to cross for yourself' said my little book. Easy enough on foot but too rocky and boggy for the pony. I began to feel anxious. Leaving Susanne reluctantly holding Peggy, I went ahead to check out possible routes. Two months earlier I wouldn't have hesitated to take a pony down this marshy path but now the sight and squelching sound of bog – even relatively firm bog like this – brought back hideous memories and a surge of adrenalin.

I returned to Susanne. Peggy was walking restlessly in circles, pawing the ground and snatching at tufts of bog grass. "She's a crazy horse!" said Susanne. "She didn't like you going away so she started to eat the earth." Sure enough Peggy's mouth was muddy. I suggested that this time Susanne should look for a safe route while I stayed with Peggy. A track led down to the river;

although marshy and rutted it seemed firm enough and there was an easy river crossing, but it ended in a bog where turf-cutters had recently been busy. I asked her to beckon me over if there was a safe way round the turf-cutting area. Peggy was bent on demonstrating the inadequacy of her lunch. She dug at the soft soil with her forefeet and grabbed mouthfuls of dirt. "It's no good," I told her. "You're stuck with me and this is how it is."

Through the binoculars I could watch Susanne carefully checking possible routes round the bog, and then two figures caught my eye: tourists walking along the skyline, evidently on firm ground. Susanne waved and I led Peggy down the squelchy track, my heart lurching in fright each time she sank above her hooves. However, after such a long spell of dry weather, the ground was basically firm and Susanne's route gave us no trouble. By the time we reached the road my confidence was at least partially restored. It was so much easier and safer with two of us.

Peggy's relief at feeling the tarmac beneath her feet was short-lived. Buoyed by our cross-country success, I suggested that we try another short cut to a road running parallel to ours across a watery valley. This time it didn't work. First I had to deal with the wire-netting fence at the head of the steep gravel track down to the valley, un-twiddling about a dozen bits of wire to let us through and then twiddling them all up again. The track ended abruptly at a ruined farm, and beyond were clumps of gorse (the dwarf variety, also known as Irish furze, and hellishly prickly) and boulders. I led Peggy who stopped at intervals with a mulish expression on her face. Susanne went on ahead and I saw her halt at a long, perfectly maintained wire fence that continued into a bog-fringed lake. There was no way round. We went our separate ways back to the road, Susanne taking a labotious cross-country route to intersect the road lower down while Peggy walked briskly back the way we'd come with little 'I told you so' snorts, and grudgingly climbed the hill towards the road. She always objected to steep hills. Believing herself equal to any car when it came to roadwork, she considered rough terrain an unfair test for a harness pony. She approached hills like an inexperienced mountain climber, racing up for a dozen or so yards, then stopping to get her breath back. I tried to educate her into the proper mountaineer's plod but she wasn't interested, preferring to think up excuses for calling a halt. She was working on another delaying tactic: stopping to evacuate her bowels. Fair enough, I thought, I wouldn't want to continue walking under those circumstances, so I let her pause. She soon learned that by squeezing her droppings out one at a time ('horse-apples' Susanne called them) she could stop as often as she wanted. By the end of the trek she'd so perfected the technique I feared she'd do herself an internal injury by straining so hard.

Susanne was wading through waist-high shrubbery towards our meeting place. Her short cut had turned out, as most short cuts do, to be longer than my route and much more arduous. She'd had enough for the first day, and I'd had enough of her wretched stripy bag which caused the saddlebags to slip to one side. We agreed that she should hitchhike to the Hennessys and I'd meet her there. I described it as best I could since, in common with most rural Irish houses, there was no name or number on the gate. She passed me, waving, after 20 minutes or so, and I arrived to find her sitting outside the bungalow. Peggy's former friend, the jennet, hopped along by the fence on its hobbled legs, squeaking its greeting, but Peggy was more interested in grass so we turned her loose into the field and went in to see the family.

ʊ ʊ ʊ

The Hennessys were in fine fettle. Kathleen repeated for Susanne's benefit the ghost story of the giant barrel thing that had rolled around Mollie's valley, trapping people in their houses until a priest performed an exorcism. And she added another:

"One night I went to check on the boys before going to bed. As I was leaving their room I heard this noise. It was a wailing, like a woman crying, but with no pause or breath. I looked out of the window. Dark as dungeons, it was, and this cry was getting nearer. I'm telling you it was like no man nor beast. It made my blood run cold. I ran in to wake Sylvester. He was 12 at the time. You remember that night, don't you Vesta? The wailing noise came closer and closer then faded away."

Fascinating! This was the banshee wailer which is supposed to presage death. The origin of the word is interesting. *Bean sídhe* in Irish is literally 'fairy woman' but the meaning goes much deeper. Underground, in fact, to the Tuatha Dé Danaan people of Irish mythology who became invisible and took up residence in the 'fairy mounds' that can still be seen in Ireland.

After the ghost stories I told of my wanderings with Peggy before Susanne's arrival and mentioned the foul-mouthed man with two horses. "We know him!" Noel exclaimed. "You could only be talking about one fellow. Remember that time he came here, Mum?" They rocked with laughter and Kathleen continued.

"I was working in the kitchen one day and there was a knock at the back door. There was that farmer, looking all wet and sad. 'Could you give me a little piece of bread?' he asked, all humble. 'I've been out in the hills all day and haven't a bite to eat!' Well of course I invited him in and put the kettle on for tea and started boiling some eggs. Then he went to the door and shouted, 'It's OK boys, the kettle's on and she's boiling eggs,' and eight men appeared!"

The family spluttered with laughter. "Do you remember the shoe business?" Kathleen was too convulsed at the memory to continue. Sylvester took up the story.

"You see he damaged his shoe. Tore the sole away and it couldn't be mended. So he found a shop in Limerick that had the very same pair in the window. He went in and said, 'I've got a friend outside in the car and poor man he's only got one leg. He can't come in himself but he takes the same size as me so can I just try them?' Then he said, 'He'll only need one. Can I take it out so he can try it?' And of course that was the last the shop saw of him!"

Story time was cut short by the failing light. We had to set up camp in Peggy's field. My tiny tent was designed for a single person or couples as chummy as well-ripened peas in a pod. To give ourselves a little more room we pitched only the fly and hoped the weather would stay dry. It looked as though the cloudless days we'd enjoyed since my return to Ireland would last forever, but the weatherman had predicted thunderstorms.

It didn't rain and we both slept well so one minor anxiety about our trip together could be dispensed with, although mostly we planned to use hostels and B&Bs. Kathleen's story-telling continued over breakfast. I wanted to hear about life in Ireland in the old days. "When I was a girl they were mostly arranged marriages. It was important for the girl to have a fortune. She couldn't make a good marriage if she couldn't bring some money to the husband's household, so most girls left school at 14 and went to America to work as servants. They came back with their fortune and married a boy their parents had chosen. Only the eldest son stayed on the farm. The others had to find work somewhere else. Often they went to England. So a girl with a good fortune could marry a farmer and live with the husband's parents. Young people didn't have their own house in those days."

I reflected that times hadn't changed much; most of the households I'd visited had the eldest son working on the farm and living with his parents. If none of the sons had married they usually continued to live at home.

◡　◡　◡

I was concerned at the state of Peggy's shoes. The set that Pedar had provided were half-worn when he put them on, and now they were very thin and her hooves overgrown. Pedar had rather airily told me you could buy horseshoes in the pub in Dingle, but I'd never pursued that option. Noel said there was a blacksmith on the road towards the village of Camp, so we decided to pay him a visit after our planned frolic on the beach.

The beach was a seven-mile stretch of sand facing Brandon Bay. After doing seaside stuff our plan was that I would gallop away along the length of the strand to Rough Point at the tip of the finger of land that poked north into the Atlantic, and then head inland to Camp while Susanne returned to the road to hitchhike to the blacksmith where we'd meet. Peggy walked gingerly onto the sand, snorting in anxiety, but she was braver than her first time on Ventry Strand. I noticed with approval that her head carriage was becoming almost normal and she no longer peeped under those imaginary blinkers. Finding a spot away from the staring families, we removed the saddlebags and took it in turn to ride. I had a gallop and Susanne had a jog trot while I watched anxiously, expecting Peggy to take off at any moment. Peggy behaved impeccably. Susanne walked further along the beach with her, turned, and to my alarm I saw Peggy break into a canter with Susanne bouncing and wobbling, but staying aboard. She pulled up wreathed in smiles. "That was fantastic! Why are you looking so worried? I galloped!"

We changed into our swimsuits and took it in turns to have a dip while Peggy pranced around excitedly digging holes in the sand with her forefoot. I thought it was time that she learned the delights of sea bathing. Swimming with Mollie had been one of the highlights of the group trek I'd taken with Willy Leahy before setting off on my own. Peggy reluctantly agreed to go as far as the surf, and even to let the waves break over her legs, but spun round every time I urged her to go deeper. I nearly fell off, and agreed that she'd been very brave and had done enough for the day.

Our plan for going our separate ways was a failure. Susanne's luggage, too awkward for her to carry with her, was insecurely attached to the saddle and prevented me from galloping. Indeed, it prevented me from riding at all since I couldn't get it properly balanced and the saddlebags constantly slipped to one side, or the stripy bag fell off. I was livid. Fuming, I led Peggy up the beach to the next access road, stopping frequently to push the bags back into position, curse Susanne, and glare at people who stared. It took a couple of hours to reach the forge where I found Susanne in no better humour. After waiting for an hour for a lift she'd been picked up by a man who 'wouldn't keep his hands with him'. Then, having located the blacksmith she was told that he didn't shoe horses these days.

Susanne and I were hardly speaking. She, sensibly, was keeping silent until I was in a better mood, and I was still furious over being denied a gallop because of her bag. I also had not forgiven her for that morning's observation that Peggy was stupid. "Stupid! She's the most intelligent pony I've ever known! That's the problem." Peggy had refused to be caught when we'd packed up the tent and were ready to leave. Over the last week she had learned that the day didn't end with her returning home to Dingle and her equine friends, and that she was expected to cope with all sorts of unreasonable challenges and spend each night in unfamiliar surroundings. No wonder her enthusiasm for the job was dwindling.

We all needed something to eat. Opposite the forge was an elegant gateway behind a triangle of very green lawn grass. Tying Peggy with the long rope to a side gate so she could get full benefit of this excellent grazing, Susanne and I settled down to our picnic and the map. Killarney was the next destination but the priority was to get Peggy shod and I knew where to go. My favourite family in Ireland lived the other side of the peninsula at Castlemaine. Dinny O'Shea had shod Mollie just before her accident and I wanted the family to meet Peggy. Our one-walk-one-ride method of travelling was not really working; Susanne had blisters from the previous day and there seemed little we could do to solve the luggage problem. We had to rethink our plans.

Our discussion was abruptly halted by a commotion from Peggy, who was plunging around with her head tucked into her chest. I knew immediately what had happened: her tether rope had caught round her back leg. I'd seen Mollie go through the same struggle by the Cliffs of Moher. Would I never learn? By the time I'd picked myself up (I'd been knocked down by the suddenly tightened rope) Peggy was standing motionless, trussed like a fowl, her head pulled sideways against her shoulder, waiting for help. She remained still while I fumbled with the buckle of her head collar and once she was out of her predicament she started eating again as though nothing had happened. However, I was mortified to find she'd sustained a nasty rope burn on the fleshy upper part of her hind leg. Pedar had told me that Peggy was not accustomed to being tethered. It was something else she would need to be taught.

We both made much of Peggy. Susanne commented how sensible she had been to stop struggling and wait for help, even though the position she had to wait in must have been painfully uncomfortable, and I immediately forgave her the earlier thoughtless remark. "Yes, ponies are much more sensible than horses. Thank goodness."

The yellowish-grey clouds that had been building up during the day broke in the predicted thunderstorm as we continued east. Cringing under our waterproofs, the idea of camping near the top of the pass no longer appealed and we started looking out for B&B signs. Usually they seem to grow like grass by the road but we'd hit an arid patch. Susanne went into a small post office to buy stamps and ask about accommodation. "You won't find one around here," said the post mistress cheerfully. We did find one around there, however, once we'd turned up the mountain road. The woman looked doubtfully at Peggy. "Sure you could tie her out there but what would the pet lamb think?" The pet lamb was a large and woolly sheep tethered by a leg on a grassy slope. The woman directed us to the proprietor of a restaurant who provided accommodation for caravan horses. Leaving Susanne to haul the luggage to our room, I trotted bareback up the road under a yellow sky and soon Peggy was happily sniffing at caravan-horse droppings in a large and pricey field. Later we had a large and pricey – and outstanding – meal at the restaurant, feeling guilty at the extravagance but, after all, Susanne was on holiday and we'd all had a tough day.

Chapter 3

We struggled with the errant bag one more time as we crossed the peninsula via the Caherconree mountain road between Camp and Aughils. The thunderstorm had only taken the edge off the heat and it was still very warm. Taking it in turns to ride, we ambled past cultivated land and a scattering of houses shaded by trees until the abrupt line where mountain and moorland took over. The heather was just starting to come into flower, and splashes of mauve punctuated the green bracken and grass up the hillsides. As we climbed to the top of the pass there were only sheep to observe our passing. No cars. We could have been hundreds of miles from the nearest town. Near the summit are the remains of an Iron-Age fort which was supposedly occupied by Cú Roí Mac Dairi, a giant who had the handy knack of rotating his fortress by remote control after sundown so that wherever he was in the world – and he was a great traveller – his enemies could never find the entrance. Unfortunately he hadn't taken into account the treachery of his wife, who poured milk into the river to indicate that he was at home, so he finally met a sticky end.

Our plan was that we would split up once we reached the main road that runs along the southern part of the peninsula. Susanne would hitch to

Killarney and do touristy stuff for two days and I would follow after my visit to the blacksmith. First we had to phone the Aghadoe hostel, one of Ireland's most popular, to make sure they had room and check that there was somewhere for Peggy. Here, at least, was a hostel with a phone, but finding a phone box was a challenge. Eventually I was directed to a private house where, for some reason, they had a coin box in the conservatory. "Tomorrow, did you say? If you get here by 5 o'clock you should get a bunk." I explained about Peggy. "There's a big lawn in front of the house where I suppose you can tether her. But I don't want her eating the flowers." I assured him that Peggy's botanical interest was limited to grass, and that I would be make sure I arrived in Killarney in good time.

I left Susanne sitting rather forlornly beside a pile of luggage on the side of the road, and trotted briskly to Castlemaine, stopping to have a sandwich and ice cream at an outdoor café. I was still wary about leaving Peggy tied up because of her propensity for demolishing fences.

U   U   U

A warm welcome awaited me when I reached the O'Sheas' in the early evening. The family had heard about Mollie's death and Beth told me that 12-year-old Anthony had taken it very hard. "I'm sure we could have done something to help, to prevent it happening," he'd said. As before, within moments of arriving I was sitting in front of a huge meal while Peggy had her old shoes taken off and her feet pared down. Then the family went off to watch one of the sons play football and Peggy and I were shown to Uncle Denny's acre where he had lived before moving in with his brother. It was still quite early so I leaned against a haystack in the sun and watched Peggy learn about tethers.

Before setting out with Mollie I had ordered a single-stake hobble from America, and used to tether her by a foreleg to a sort of giant corkscrew which was light-weight but held securely in the ground. It was never entirely satisfactory. Although Mollie eventually got the hang of it, the radius between the stake and Mollie's munching mouth was too small. Rethinking the geometry of it, I realised that by tethering the pony from a back leg we got the additional length of Peggy's body so more grazing area. There was also the advantage that when the chain tightened it would be behind her. And the weight of the chain kept it on the ground so she wouldn't get tangled up as she had with the rope.

It worked perfectly. It took Peggy a while to learn that she could move around safely with this thing on her leg, and she was certainly quite cross about it, but by dusk she was grazing with her hind leg outstretched, at the end of her tether literally and metaphorically. I then turned her loose – the field was enclosed so this was just a preliminary lesson.

The haystack was probably not the best choice of back rest; I spent the next couple of days picking ticks off myself. I had set the tent up but never slept in it; Denny's neighbour Mary came across and invited me for a cup of tea, and we found so much to talk about that I ended up going to bed in her caravan at 2 o'clock. Our conversation began with Mary asking if I had any children. Normally in Ireland I'm reticent about my former marital status since I knew that divorce was illegal, but I explained that my childless state was by choice. "Oh yes, divorce is very straightforward in England," I said when she questioned me further. "After we'd been separated for two years it was by mutual consent." Mary, haltingly, told me her story.

Her husband had left her for another woman when their daughter was small. She felt utterly isolated, knowing no other single mothers and without her own transport. There was no bus service into Tralee where she might have met other women in a similar situation. Then the local priest preached a sermon on the wickedness of broken marriages. "I felt that terrible. Everyone in the village knew that he was pointing his finger at me."

With immense courage she went to see the priest and explained her circumstances. "And you know what? Next Sunday he preached about the wickedness of husbands who desert their wives!" This may have made living in a small town a little easier, but Mary's house legally belonged to her husband so she couldn't sell it without his permission. She was stuck. And yet she still didn't believe in divorce. She wasn't alone in this. When Ireland held a referendum in 1986, the proposal to remove the ban on divorce was rejected by a large majority. It wasn't until 1994 that the electorate accepted a change in the law.

By the time I'd got the tent packed up next morning, Peggy was wearing new shoes and a smug expression. Then Mary's little daughter had her first-ever pony ride and loved it, and Anthony got on and showed that he could ride much better than me, even holding the puppy in front of him on the saddle. I loaded up the saddlebags, everyone waved goodbye, and Peggy and I set off in the sunshine for Killarney. I was soon able to leave the main road and follow narrow back-lanes which were lined with purple loosestrife, foxgloves, knapweed and all the smells of summer.

I ate Beth's picnic by a river so that Peggy could have drink. At least she was not as fussy as Mollie who considered an offer of water from my yellow plastic bucket as attempted poisoning, but she still preferred to watch me slide down a muddy, nettle-clad bank to a stream, then refuse the water that I brought back. If I could find a pony-accessible river like this one I always took Peggy there. She was often thirsty in this hot weather.

A little way downstream was a boy fishing. He walked up for a chat and to boast that he had caught an 8lb salmon in that same stretch of the river. "You English? I've got friends staying from Belfast. Come from the Falls Road area." I made appreciative noises. "I go up there whenever I can. We have a grand time." I asked politely what he liked so much about Belfast. "We go and throw stones at the soldiers." He went on to tell me of a gruesome shooting his friends had witnessed and I tried not to feel personally to blame for Northern Ireland.

At Aghadoe Heights at the top of the pass above Lough Leane, I saw why Killarney is so popular with visitors. Spread out in front of me was the lake, blue as the ocean, encircled by forested headlands and backed by MacGillycuddy's Reeks, a mountain range impressive by any standard, but wonderful in this setting. If this was good, when I saw the youth hostel my mouth must have dropped open. Aghadoe House was, and still is, an elegant manor built in pinkish sandstone in the 1820s and formerly the home of Lord Headley. "In most countries if a man steals land from the natives they put him in prison. In Britain they make him a lord," explained the warden later. It was burned down in the 1920s, along with so many gracious houses belonging to the English aristocracy, but restored to its original splendour, and has been part of the Irish Youth Hostel Association, An Óige, since 1957. I arrived before it was open and sat on the spacious lawn with a dozen or so cyclists and walkers who stared in disbelief at me, my pony and my saddlebags.

U U U

While we waited, Susanne arrived having had a hugely enjoyable day. "I decided to hitchhike from the hostel to Killarney to see what the town was like. I was picked up by this lovely old priest and he said he had nothing much to do today and that he wanted to show me his country. So he took me to all sorts of interesting places, but best of all when he dropped me off at the hostel he said, 'This was the loveliest day of my life!'"

"How about yesterday?" I asked. "I felt guilty leaving you on the side of the road with all that luggage. How long did you wait?"

"Oh not too long. But I had a bit of a problem with this man. He talked a lot with his very thick Irish accent, and I couldn't understand him very well.

But then he said there was a lake nearby and wouldn't I like to see it? Perhaps a little swim because it was so hot? I thought he was acting a bit strange, so I said no. Then he said something like 'just a moment to cool off my chopper in the water' and I didn't like this at all so I told him to take me immediately to the hostel. Which he did, very apologetic."

I tethered Peggy by her back leg, twisting my corkscrew picket into the soft ground of the lawn. I'd thanked the warden profusely for this privilege. "Just keep her away from my car," he said warningly. He'd already noticed her interest. Peggy loved cars; they reminded her of the good old days when she pulled a gig. The hostel was crowded with very noisy groups of very young people, all filling the capacious kitchen with smoke from their burnt sausages and frizzled bacon. We felt quite matronly, but at least we got a bunk each; latecomers were being turned away or put on mattresses on the floor. I kept popping out to check on Peggy who was still coming to terms with her tether. One time I found she'd pulled the picket up and was making faces at herself in the warden's wing mirror. I moved her to a firmer bit of lawn, well away from temptation.

That evening I discovered I'd reached a landmark: 100 miles since first mounting Peggy in Castle Gregory. Each day I measured our mileage on the map with a length of thread, marked out in miles to the inch, which I kept tied to my diary. I still have it.

∪   ∪   ∪

We planned to stay a couple of days at the hostel and see the area properly. Susanne told me that the nicest place she'd been to with the priest was Muckross House and that she'd love to visit it again and see the inside. It was part of Killarney National Park, which is closed to vehicles, but the tourist office said that we could ride there. We needed to take Peggy out for the day since I didn't think I could leave her safely on the hostel lawn.

On our way to the park we called in on Donal O'Sullivan who ran a pony trekking centre. I wanted to make the most of the Iveragh Peninsula to the west of Killarney, and thought that he would be the best source of information for off-road routes.

"That's a grand pony for the job," said Donal, as Peggy neighed her greetings to his animals. "I'll get her some feed while we talk." He produced a bucket of special horse oats enriched with molasses which Peggy regarded with the utmost suspicion. It was possibly the first time she'd seen oats and I'd already discovered that she didn't have a sweet tooth. Sugar lumps were spurned and I hadn't been able to persuade her to eat apple cores, despite putting them in her mouth and holding it closed so she could appreciate the yummy flavour. As soon as she could, she'd spit them out. Brown bread was all this peasant would eat.

I tied her to a rail in the cowshed so she could enjoy her gourmet meal in peace while Donal and I spread out the map. "No, you won't be allowed to take the pony into the National Park," he said. "They've given me permission to take escorted groups but there are too many irresponsible tourist riders." That was a blow. What would we do with Peggy during the day? While we were considering our options there was a commotion in the cowshed and Peggy shot out backwards dragging the broken rail. That was the third bit of timber she'd broken in just over a week; I really *had* to cure her of this phobia. Despite seeing his property gradually demolished in front of his eyes, Donal offered to keep Peggy in the loosebox until the evening and then put her in a field for the night.

If oats were a possible first for Peggy, a stable almost certainly was. She stepped hesitantly into it and when I took her tack off and shut the loosebox door she put her nose over the top and looked so tragic I could hardly bring myself to leave. I felt even worse when I returned for my bag and was greeted with a 'Get me out of here!' neigh.

For the rest of the day Susanne and I behaved like ordinary tourists. We hired bicycles in Killarney which, I noted in my diary, had prostituted itself to tourism. 'It may once have been a charming town,' I wrote, 'and perhaps it regains its original character in the winter [it does], but in August we were not tempted to linger around the souvenir shops and rows of jaunting cars.'

Muckross House and its grounds, on the other hand, were unspoiled. We cycled along the narrow tracks – closed to motor traffic – and I could see for the first time why Killarney has excited visitors for so many years. No doubt the Victorians saw it at its best; Muckross House was built in 1843 in Tudor style as a sort of Irish Castle Howard, the owner, Henry Arthur Herbert, sparing no expense to make it equal to any other stately home in the Empire. He was successful. Titled visitors flocked there and left written tribute: 'There is no place which can compare with Killarney and I have seen much of the world' (Lord Castlerosse), 'I never in my life saw anything more beautiful. I might say so beautiful' (Lord Macaulay) and 'Within the circuit of a moderate day's walk [can be found] almost every possible variety of the wild, the majestic, the beautiful, the picturesque' (Lord Ritchie). Mr Herbert was an MP and his dedicated service to the Crown eventually ruined him. Queen Victoria paid a visit to Muckross in 1861 and the expense of keeping the royal party in the manner to which they were accustomed contributed to his bankruptcy. The Herbert family's association with Muckross, which had lasted two centuries, ended in 1899 when the house was sold.

The house is open year-round and I have enjoyed a recent winter visit as much as our tour of 1984. The Killarney inlaid furniture is an eye-opener, so beautiful and unique to this part of Ireland, and the huge antlers of an Irish elk, found in a local bog, are a reminder that evolution may sometimes lead to a dead end. The theory that this giant deer was made extinct by its impractical headgear seems entirely plausible. In the summer there's a folk museum and craft centre and the beautiful grounds with its lake views, fairy-tale woods with lumpy moss-covered boulders and a backdrop of mountains, can be enjoyed by all.

ᘮ   ᘮ   ᘮ

Over dinner Susanne and I planned the next section of the trek. Encouraged by the ease of hitchhiking, and gaining confidence in riding, Susanne felt that the one-walk-one-ride method was enjoyable for scenic stretches, but that she should hitch ahead on the main roads. I could then sharpen Peggy up with some trotting. We had already pared our luggage down so it all fitted in the saddlebags, leaving the unwanted stuff in storage at the youth hostel. We decided to keep our plans fluid, just focusing on one day at a time. Exploring away from the tarred roads was anyway going to be easier since the Killarney area was blessed with an inch-to-the-mile map that marked green roads and tracks. Our first goal would be the famous Gap of Dunloe, which I remembered from a family holiday in Killarney when I was a stroppy 15-year-old. Because it involved horses, it's the only bit of that holiday that I recall with any pleasure. No cars were allowed on the narrow road between the mountains. Visitors were plonked on horses – never mind if they'd never ridden before – and a little girl with a whip kept them at a brisk trot and denied the thirsty animals any water. At the end my mother had a half-crown-sized raw spot on her bottom, and never got on a horse again, whilst my father was so enthused by the experience that he signed up for riding lessons when we got home. The worst part of that holiday was the ascent of Carrantuohill, Ireland's highest mountain. The memories of loose scree and deep bog, swirling mist obscuring the views, and tears are still vivid. Even David, the spaniel, was miserable.

ᘮ   ᘮ   ᘮ

Back to the Gap of Dunloe. During the ice age a flow of rock, ice and glacial debris built up in the Black Valley, finding an outlet to the east of MacGillycuddy's Reeks and cut the deep gorge we now call the Gap of Dunloe. Three lakes were left in the wake of the receding ice, adding to the natural beauty of Ireland's most spectacular mountain pass which has been left almost untouched by the tourist industry. There's a collection of cafés and souvenir shops at the staging post known as Kate Kearney's Cottage but nothing on the mountain road itself except jaunting cars and self-willed horses with their ineffectual tourist riders. Only in the winter are cars allowed.

For nearly two centuries travellers have refreshed themselves at Kate Kearney's Cottage before setting off through the pass. Today they partake of coffee and cakes, but in Kate Kearney's time in the early part of the 19th century, it was a far more potent brew that was on offer. Kate Kearney's Mountain Dew was so 'fierce and wild, it required not less than seven times its own quantity of water to tame and subdue it'. The heady experience was no doubt helped by the fact that Kate herself was intoxicatingly beautiful. I wondered if it was Kate Kearney's Cottage that I remember from 1956. Probably not, because that little thatched cottage was notable, not for its refreshments, but for the toothless crone who hovered in the doorway. "I like to watch the motors," she told us.

I went to collect Peggy early the next morning. "She's very trusting," said Donal. "Walked right up to me when I came for her this morning." I was quite put out. I thought it was only me that she came to – when she felt like it. She was back in the stable and very relieved to be released from her prison. We trotted briskly to Aghadoe House, loaded up, and set off for the Gap of Dunloe.

Susanne and I had arranged to meet at Kate Kearney's Cottage, a distance of about five miles from the hostel. The luggage was now much lighter and

Peggy sprightly after her day's rest, so we were soon sipping tea while Peggy neighed at the other horses and nuzzled for titbits. Some of the horse-hirers came over to talk to us. "Nice mare, who does she belong to?"

"She's mine. I bought her in Dingle." There was a reason behind this lie. Donal had warned us that the close-knit community of horse-hirers did not take kindly to outsiders. "So don't say Peggy's hired or they'll give you a bad time."

"Is that so? She's very quiet." (speculative look in her mouth) "Would you be selling her now?"

"Um, yes, but not for a long time."

"I'll buy her. I can pick her up in the truck when you finish your ride."

"Oh, she's not suitable. She coughs and there's something wrong with her leg. Besides, her previous owner wants to buy her back. Yes, he said he wants first refusal…" I floundered on but in the end had to accept the man's name and address. Even if Peggy had been mine, no way would I have submitted her to the drudgery of trotting up and down that same road each day.

∪   ∪   ∪

It was another hot day. The sun shone on the rumps of drooping horses awaiting their tourist riders for the journey over the pass and back, but there were few visitors around when we set out along the white dirt road. Every now and then a jaunting car would trot by, but otherwise we had the pass to ourselves. The route deserves its reputation. The green and grey mountains crouched over the road, with their detritus carelessly dropped at their feet. Great rocks, the size of bungalows, had come to rest by the road, or were halted in their descent in gulleys or on ledges. Sheep picked at the grass which remained green despite the drought, and the sun brought deep shadows across the valley.

We picnicked at a bridge where the road crosses the River Loe before it broadens into the first lake. It was a windless day, just a faint breeze wobbling the reflections in the lake. We were in no hurry to continue, but Peggy was in a tiresome mood; instead of grazing she paced up and down until I tethered her, which caused yells of anger from passing horse-hirers who assumed, reasonably enough, that we were irresponsible tourists with a loose horse. After the third lake the pass narrows, the road zigzagging up between steep black cliffs to Head of Gap with its views over the Black Valley and Purple Mountain, though in a few weeks' time this would be coloured with heather; the name derives from the purplish tinge of the rocks.

At the Black Valley there were decisions to be made. A youth hostel at the foot of the pass had looked inviting on the map but it was too soon to stop for the night. Every day we expected the perfect weather to break. We continued west along the valley, splitting up so that Susanne could take a short cut along a footpath marked on the map. I'd been tempted to ride it but a woman emerged from a cottage, peering at us in amazement, and advised us not to take Peggy. "'Tis awful rough."

Susanne was waiting for me where her footpath rejoined the road: "Hilary, you must look at the horses of that man over there. They're beautiful! He told me about them but I couldn't understand." (Susanne speaks excellent English but had a hard time, as I did, getting to grips with the Kerry accent.) I followed her directions down a grassy track and through a broken gate to a half-derelict cottage sitting damply under a high bank. An old man with a greasy peaked cap turned back to front and manure-coloured clothes was stacking turf. He greeted me enthusiastically. "It's my horses you'll be wanting is it? Let me show you." He didn't need to show me, I'd already seen two of them as they grazed near the cottage. They would not have looked out of place in the show ring. There was a jet-black gelding that shone in the evening sun, and two chestnut mares as plump and glossy as conkers. But the one that had caught Susanne's eye was milk-white with a pink nose and hooves. "I look after 'em well," the old man said with satisfaction when I expressed my admiration.

I asked him about an enticing-looking footpath which the map showed as connecting our valley with the neighbouring one. It climbed to a pass and the closeness of the contour lines indicated a steep but not impossible drop down to the next valley. Could we safely take Peggy over? "Oh you'll get over there all right," he said rather too airily. "And you could camp anywhere in this valley. No-one lives there now. Plenty of good fields for your pony, or you could come in with me," he added, twinkling, his three teeth showing in a dark banana-shaped grin. "I'm all alone."

At the head of the valley, just before the pass, we found the most idyllic campsite of the whole trip. The track led us through several well-fenced fields empty of livestock but with plenty of lush grass watered by a small stream. We turned Peggy loose in the field that sloped down to the stream and set up our tent in the adjoining one. A large, flat-topped rock served as a table and the river, running into deep pools, as a bath. The water was almost tepid after its journey over sun-warmed rocks and the evening hot and still. I'm not one for leaping into every icy mountain stream with squeals of delight, but this was different. It was heavenly. We'd stocked up with food in Killarney so could indulge in tinned stew mixed with packet soup and midges, followed by yoghurt, fruit, and coffee. We climbed into our sleeping bags well-fed, clean, and in love with Ireland.

☾   ☾   ☾

When I went to check on Peggy first thing the next morning, I found her lying down, dozing in the sun. I'd never seen her so relaxed, and was happy to leave her in peace while I checked out the pass on foot. The way up was marked with white-painted posts, which took a rough but dry route. I followed it to the highest point where the view was breathtaking: my nemesis all those years ago, Carrantuohill, loomed above me on the right, the clouds already gathering on its summit to confuse any climbers. In front was the green Caragh River valley disappearing into the haze and bordered on each side by steep mountains. I desperately wanted to go over this pass but without putting Peggy at any risk. The route down was certainly steep: I followed the white posts through bracken and boulders. It was these boulders that worried me; Peggy would have to pick her way very carefully. Yet she was a sensible pony and I'd seen horses and mules cope with worse in the Andes during the decade that I worked as a trek leader.

Susanne had the tent packed up when I returned. I reported on the situation. "As I see it we have three choices: we go back and round by the road; you go over the pass on your own and I'll meet you tonight; or we all go over if Peggy is sensible." We looked at the map. Going round would add a further 11 miles. We looked at Peggy, well-fed and content and oh so sensible, and decided we'd give it a go. If she made heavy weather of the ascent then we'd turn back; the descent into the next valley would be much harder. Peggy was in an exceptionally obliging mood, following us willingly as we led her along the track and up the rocky slope to the pass. She jumped up steep places and placed her hooves carefully between the rocks. She would be all right; I gave her a rest at the top and made a fuss of her before we started down the other side. It was not easy. Peggy soon lost her enthusiasm and stopped every few minutes to force out a horse-apple. I couldn't blame her; the route indicated by the white posts was fine for walkers, taking them boulder-hopping down the mountain, but we had to try to find alternative Peggy-routes where she wouldn't slip on the rocks on her new shoes. Our progress was very slow. Susanne had to go ahead and find the best route and then return to be ready to drive Peggy forward if she did her mulish act and refused to be led. At least we had a good supply of brown bread as a reward for particularly accomplished slides and jumps.

We dropped 700 feet in less than half a mile and looking back at the steep rock-strewn hillside from the safety of the track at the bottom, it seemed incredible that Peggy had made such a descent. Our praise was effusive, but our relief premature. The marked path led to a stile over a well-made wire fence. There was no way round; we were stuck. Peggy grazed while we considered our situation. When we'd met the track at the foot of the hill we'd turned right, since the other way would have taken us to the wrong side of the valley. Scanning our route through binoculars from the top of the pass I had noted that this track apparently ended at a farmhouse, but perhaps it continued and joined the road we could see beyond the house. A few fields away a shepherd was busy with his sheep. I had no difficulty deciding which of us should go over and ask directions. I watched through binoculars as Susanne climbed the stile and made her way towards him. I could see her gestures and hear two voices but no words. I could tell that the meeting was not going well. Susanne turned and started back up the hill followed by angry-shepherd sounds. She arrived considerably shaken. "He said if he catches anyone tampering with his fence he'll shoot the person and the horse," she reported.

We nervously followed the track ending at the farmhouse, keeping an eye on the shepherd bellowing at his sheepdog below us and expecting any minute to feel a bullet in our backs. We were summoning the courage to open the farmyard gate when a man suddenly appeared. "It's him!" whispered Susanne in a frightened voice. But he was smiling broadly as he opened the gate. "Maybe it's his brother." Not a close brother at any rate since he was quite exceptionally friendly, racing on ahead to open the gates and chattering the while about ponies and tourists and the drought.

We'd made the right choice. A good track led us across the valley to the road. We stopped for lunch by the river and unloaded Peggy so she could have a much-deserved rest and feed before continuing west along Bridia Valley towards Glencar.

When we reached a sign for the Mountain Hut, an independent hostel, we were tempted to stop. But it was only 3 o'clock on a warm afternoon; it was too early and too lovely to call it a day. A woman came towards us carrying a heavy shopping bag. She lived at the house the other side of the wire fence and its stile (with, we learned later, her son the angry shepherd). "We don't have a car right now," she said. "I get transport at the end of the road." What transport could she get? I wondered. I was sure there were no buses. After walking the three miles from her house to the road she probably had to wait for a friend to drive by. She was glad to put the bag down and chat. Full of admiration that Peggy had come over the pass, she then said, "But why didn't you take the higher route near the lake? It would have brought you out behind the house, and there are no rocks!"

Chapter 4

Susanne was disgusted. "I think these awful Germans must be part of a disadvantaged youth programme. I'm glad there's no room!" It was Peggy who made the decision to stop at the Climbers' Inn. She raised her head, pricked her ears and let out a long, echoing neigh. All the windows shot open, heads poked out and the German equivalent of "Good grief!" accompanied the sound of footsteps clattering down the stairs. After we'd politely answered questions (in English, Susanne refused to reveal that she was German) and learned that there was no room at the inn, we fled to a nearby B&B. It was all shiny Wonderboard and fresh paint, run by an implausibly young couple who seem surprised to find themselves in charge of a guesthouse. We suspected that it was a wedding present from Dad. A plaster statuette of Jesus had pride of place in the lounge, gazing anxiously at his bleeding heart as though thinking 'How will I explain it to Mum? It'll never wash out!'

I thought a pub called The Climbers' Inn would be full of tourists in knee breeches, hairy socks and boots, but when we returned for a drink in the evening we found we were the only visitors. I had also thought that a pub in the heart of Kerry would be self-consciously Irish, but it was wholly delightful. There were very few women; most of the customers were old men with gnarled faces, reminiscent of a German woodcut, and cloth caps. We were delighted to recognise our smiling friend from the valley, the antidote to the 'I'll shoot the person and the horse' farmer. We learned that he was no relation to his neighbour ("His mother's awful hard on him," he explained, when we hesitatingly told our story about the gun) and that his name was Jimmy. He was so thrilled to have not one, but two ladies talking to him, that he became almost incoherent. His blue eyes wandered independently round the room and his grin got wider and wider showing a scant but serviceable number of teeth. We mischievously asked him if he was married. "Dear God no, oh Lord no, who'd have me? All I can hope for now is an old'un; I can keep her warm in the winter." Delighted laughter all round. Jimmy had a friend called John, very old and tiny and completely toothless, and took great pains to include him in the conversation and explain everything. More and more men joined us, complaining that women were in short supply since no one wanted to live in their isolated valley. One of the younger ones looked wistfully at Susanne. "What about all those ladies in Germany? Could you send them over to marry us?"

One of the old men, Michael, produced an accordion and rather pensively started playing. No-one took much notice. Jimmy tried to persuade us to dance and I wished later that we had; an Irish bar is no place to be inhibited. It was by far our nicest pub evening. Nights out in Dingle and Killarney had produced a tourist menu of over-amplified popular songs and easily-resisted inducements to merriment.

ʊ   ʊ   ʊ

We were heading, eventually, to Waterville at the end of the Iveragh Peninsula, so were enthused when the manager of the inn, Jack Walsh, told us of an old 'butter road' going over the nearby mountains which would be far more interesting than the road shown on our map. In the olden days men used to carry firkins of butter along these lanes to the ports; in this case presumably Waterville. A firkin held 56lbs of butter. Needless to say the old road was just off our very good inch-to-the-mile map covering the Killarney district (sod's law: all interesting places are on the edge of, or just off, the map) but we thought we could see an alternative access through forestry land. "Well, you might as well try," he said, so we did. First we needed to stock up with provisions and so I tied Peggy to a metal post by a petrol pump and shop. "Fill her up, please," I was going to say if someone came out. That plan was pre-empted when she did her 'Guinness for strength' act, but instead of the post breaking, the heavy-duty metal clip at the end of her extra-strong nylon lead rope snapped clean in half. I looked at the two pieces in amazement and speculated on the pounds of pull needed to break a metal clip. With that strength, I told her, she could jolly well carry me and my luggage and like it.

From Glencar we went briefly north, crossing the River Caragh at Blackstones Bridge, and passing through splendidly dramatic scenery of lake and mountain, before plunging into the pine forest to follow a track which continued encouragingly into open, rather desolate country very similar to Dartmoor. We could see a farm at the end and what looked like a path contouring round the mountains beyond, so were incredulous when the farmer and his family said they knew of no old road over the hills. We'd come at least six miles along that track and were less than a mile, as Pegasus flies, from the road to Waterville. Never liking to take no for an answer, I left Susanne and Peggy gloomily nibbling at their lunch under gathering clouds and climbed to the top of the nearby hill to see if it really was impassable. It was. Boggy with clumps of tussock grass interlaced with squelchy sheep tracks. Although I could see the Waterville road from the top, there was no sign of the butter road which should have been just below me.

So we had to go back the way we had come. These days, when good walking maps of Ireland are readily available and long-distance trails clearly marked, it's hard to convey the frustration of exploring the country with half-inch-to-the-mile maps and no system of bridle paths. I would have so loved to get off the roads on to reliable, obstacle-free tracks, but it was always a hit-or-miss experience.

When we reached the forest we succumbed to temptation and followed an inviting-looking path lined with foxgloves and heather, which ought, we thought, to meet our road and cut off a five-mile loop. It did, but the last hundred yards were across a small footbridge over a stream with steep boggy banks followed by a stile over a high wire fence. I felt close to tears. At least Susanne could continue; I had to go back. We arranged to meet in an hour and a half, which meant Peggy and I had to get a move on. At first she was happy to canter back along the path, but once on the road and asked to trot she did everything she could think of to indicate that we should stop for the night. She ostentatiously sought out grass verges for her poor tired feet, turned into fields that offered good grazing, spooked along shying at imaginary horrors and stopped to force out horse-apples. We passed a field where a lovely black pony with a head like a chess piece trotted along the fence to greet us. Peggy gave it a 'woe is me, I'm so lonely and ill-treated' neigh and it obligingly jumped out to join her, whereupon she squealed and kicked. Really, horses behave so unreasonably at times. I was not pleased to find myself with a loose pony frisking about on the road, but fortunately it belonged to the house adjacent to the field and its owner cheerfully retrieved it when he heard our hoof beats on the drive.

When I reached our meeting place at a settlement enticingly named Knocknagapple, there was no sign of Susanne. I eventually found her talking to a farmer. He hadn't heard of the butter road either but, to Peggy's obvious relief, said we could camp in his field. She made a great demonstration of chomping ravenously around the tent while I wrote my diary, ramming home her complaint about how hungry and tired she had been. She ran away with a horse's equivalent of a snarl when I went to pat her. With her interest in cars she should have been ecstatic; the farmer's son collected dead cars the way other boys collect stamps and the field was full of them. While we were sorting out our stuff a flock of sheep burst through, over and under the gate. There were many lambs looking bigger than their mothers in their thick woolly coats, but still suckling energetically. I watched a pair of gigantic twins go one on each side of a little shorn ewe who was lifted right off the ground by their efforts.

The trouble with lush grassy fields is midges. After more than two weeks of sunshine, the skies were overcast and happy dancing insects sought out our bare arms. So we were pleased to accept the offer to cook our supper in the kitchen, sneak a look at the Los Angeles Olympic Games on TV, and chat to the family. The daughter told us she worked in a bar-cum-draper. What? Oh bars were very rarely just bars in Ireland, she said, they were hardware shops, grocers, drapers… The shop assistant had to be able to pull a pint or cut a yard.

The farmer told us this story: A friend was complaining that a dog was savaging his sheep. "It's your own dog," said his neighbour.

"Impossible, I lock him in the shed each night."

"OK, just watch that shed tonight."

The farmer set up watch and saw his sheepdog jump out of the shed's open window, kill a sheep, wash itself off in the river and jump back into the shed. It sounded far-fetched, but Noel Hennessy had told me a similar tale. He'd seen his own dog disappear up the hill after a sheep, creep by with blood on its muzzle and slink off for a swim in the river before re-appearing with a 'just a little business to attend to' expression on its face.

ʊ   ʊ   ʊ

I could tell from looking at the map that the road to Waterville would be beautiful, following the River Inny through low hills and forests. But it would be a long day for Peggy, 20 miles, though easy going with some promising-looking stretches of the old road shown on the map. Everyone knew that it existed; no-one knew how much was usable now. Peggy and I had gone 17 miles that day, very little of it in the right direction.

Shortly after dawn the next morning I heard a grunting sound and looked out of the tent to see Peggy rolling energetically in the dewy grass before getting to her feet to start grazing. She knew the morning routine now, and wanted to fill her stomach before we packed up the tent. The clouds of the previous night had cleared, and the low sun outlined Peggy in gold and picked out a silver blanket of dew-covered spiders' webs covering the meadow. In this sort of weather, camping was sublime.

Once underway, our first bit of excitement was a sheep dip. A very cheerful affair for everyone but the sheep. The children sat on the wall of the corral in the sun, border collies crouched by the tightly packed flock and brawny men threw the sheep in one by one, pushing their heads under the frothy brown liquid. Emboldened by being two onlookers, not one, we stayed and chatted for a while. When I was on my own I'd passed sheep shearers without daring to stop; the cheerful togetherness of the men was too intimidating. American tourists, of course, step right in and get their legs pulled. I'd heard descriptions of what Paddy or Michael had told the video cameras about quaint Irish customs.

The grassy banks and stone walls were speckled and striped with flowers: foxgloves were still in bloom, as was purple loosestrife, knapweed and scabious. Blackberries were ripening on the roadside brambles and early hazel nuts promised a good autumn harvest. In contrast to England, where the grass verges and hedges are savagely cut back as soon as they reach their flowery best, I saw very little verge-cutting in Ireland. Too many lanes, probably. Later in the trek I met a huge hedge-trimming machine jammed along a grassy track. I was standing with Peggy in a gateway waiting for it to pass and peeping nervously round the overgrown hedge at the large man striding towards me with blazing eyes. I was sure he was going to tell me I was on private land. "Is this a main road?" he demanded.

"Well, er, no…," I faltered, waiting for the abuse.

"Then I'm lost!"

The road climbed up to the pass then dropped down to the long valley full of conifers and horseflies. Poor Peggy was driven mad by the flies but I daren't frighten her again by using the aerosol. We picked bracken fronds and fanned her head and neck as we hurried on to an attractive bridge across the river. Here we found our first stretch of butter road. At first it was a surfaced road serving a few houses, then a track, then a ghost of a track discernible by the banks that bordered a gorse-covered meadow. Then we came to a dead end: a stone wall. Not again! We were just about to turn back when an exceptionally handsome young farmer with a full set of teeth materialised out of nowhere. Sizing up the situation he removed the top stones from the wall, Peggy obligingly jumped over, we simpered our thanks and rejoined the road again, positively triumphant at having achieved a scant three-mile section of ancient road.

After that it was a question of following the river valley, crisscrossing the Inny over picturesque old bridges. The scenery became calmer, the hills lower, and the farms more prosperous-looking. Peggy kept herself amused by following close behind the person on foot and shoving her with her nose.

A gate stood open into a grassy field by the river, and I thought we could all do with a snack. We'd had an early lunch with scant grazing for Peggy. I took out her bit and let her munch away while we ate our biscuits. A very old man hobbled over, leaning on a stick, followed slowly by a very old dog. He chatted about the weather, the possibility of the drought ending that night, and what a nice pony we had. "Um. . . are we on your land?" I asked.

"That you are. I was wondering about my bull…"

We decided it was time we moved on.

ʊ   ʊ   ʊ

Susanne found a good spot for hitchhiking, and Peggy and I continued in a dreamy state, lulled by the straight road and lack of decisions. The day was cool and breezy with fluffy clouds in a blue sky. The haze of the last week had gone, leaving clear views of the layers of hills beside and behind us: green, then grey, then a distant blue. Reaching Waterville I found Susanne sitting on a wall a couple of miles from the town. With rain forecast we had decided to treat ourselves to a night indoors and we guessed that this popular town – a traditional stop on the Ring of Kerry circuit – would be full of tourist facilities. In the centre, yes, but not on the outskirts. We had a long search before we found a B&B for ourselves and a spacious field for Peggy.

Then – and now – Waterville was a typical Irish seaside town, though one with the added attraction of a large lake, Lough Currane, behind it. Rows of cheerfully painted terraced houses face a pebble beach, and there are neon signs announcing the attractions, and strolling couples down at the waterfront. A statue of Charlie Chaplin commemorates this famous visitor. Once upon a time, though, it had some even more important visitors: the boat that arrived in the harbour carried Noah's son and granddaughter plus another 49 women and two men. Some say that they set sail before the Flood, and others that in a fit of pique Noah excluded his son Bith from the ark and that Bith's daughter, Cessair, learned from supernatural sources that Ireland was free from serpents, monsters and the like (yes, I know that puts paid to the St Patrick legend – and most other legends) so would be a safe refuge from the Flood. Safe it may have been, and paradise for a while since the women were divided up among the three men, but things soon went wrong; Bith and another man died, and the remaining one, Fintan, fled and turned himself into a one-eyed salmon which served him well when Ireland was under water. Later, he metamorphosed into an eagle and eventually back into a human, becoming Fintan the Wise. But I've never quite got to grips with Irish mythology; another source tells me that at the time of the Great Flood, Ireland was inhabited by giants and monsters (the fomoire), so would hardly be the secure haven sought by Cessair. Perhaps her supernatural source got it wrong. Fintan the one-eyed salmon would have fitted right in with this crowd, some of whom had one eye, some one leg, some a goat's head and so on.

A new incarnation of the Flood began the next day. We woke to rain lashing against our window and Susanne, shocked at this introduction, after 16 days of almost unbroken sunshine, to Ireland's traditional climate, said she was not doing any more riding. Not until the rain stopped, anyway. We spread the map over the remains of our full Irish breakfast, and worked out what to do with her remaining time. Only a few days were left before she had to catch her plane back to Munich. Valentia Island was the obvious choice. It was only about 15 miles from Waterville and linked to the mainland by a bridge. "If you start now you'll get there in time to find us somewhere to stay," I said pragmatically. But first we went together to collect Peggy.

Perhaps the fomoire had got at Peggy during the night and whispered insurrection in her ear. To my astonishment, instead of walking up to me when I went into the field she trotted away and it was soon obvious that she had no intention of being caught. "Stupid horse," muttered Susanne, heading back to the B&B. Leaving Peggy eating busily, one ear cocked in my direction, I knocked on the door of the farmhouse and explained my problem to the farmer. "Like that is it? I can give you a bucket of horse nuts. That should do it." Indeed, Peggy's greed got the better of her and I was able to catch hold of her head collar. But instead of the lovely calm pony I had got used to, she was overwrought. She wouldn't let me touch her neck and started to pull back as soon as I tried to tie her to the gate so I could return the bucket. "What is it, Peggy old girl?" I asked. She and I had got to know each other pretty well during the previous three weeks and I generally knew what she was trying to communicate, but I couldn't tell if something had frightened her during the night or whether she was just being naughty.

The rain was coming in wind-driven spasms and Susanne was disenchanted with horse management and anxious to get going. Peggy was just anxious. She pranced and danced down Waterville's main street, shying at everything and making a scene about the rain. I discovered that she was even worse than Mollie in this respect, trying to face away from the wind and tensing her body against the watery lashes and exhibiting such misery that I forgot my own discomfort. My original plans to short-cut along the beach came to nothing because in her current mood I daren't ask Peggy to ford the mouth of the River Inny, so I had a long stretch of main road with plenty of traffic. Earlier in the ride Peggy had demonstrated that she had a thing about bridges and would make a fuss about crossing even wide ones. On reaching the Inny Bridge she stopped dead and stared in terror at the water on each side of the metal railings, before retreating backwards at a run in front of startled coach drivers and their passengers.

After the bridge I was able to get off the main road but she was no calmer. Shying violently at some imaginary horror she slipped and went down on her knees. With visions of Black Beauty and 'broken knees' I jumped off, sick with foreboding, expecting to see blood. But she was unhurt. I led her for a while after that and she started to quieten down.

Abandoning my plan for a scenic ride round the coast, I took the most direct route to Valentia across the peninsula in improving weather. The relentless grey of the sky started to break up allowing occasional glimpses of blue. Selecting a suitably succulent grass verge, I gave Peggy her lunch and made some damp sandwiches using the saddle as a table. My jacket, hung over a fence post, started to dry. As I led Peggy down the road a woman padded out of her cottage in bedroom slippers to have a chat. "Would you be walking all the way?" I explained that both Peggy and I needed a rest at times. "Would you like some milk? Mary, go get the lady some milk! She won't mind a mug, she's one of us." I was flattered. Not trusting her rather elegant daughter to get it right, mum trotted indoors and returned with a bottle. "It'll do you good. Fresh from the cow today."

We continued to Valentia in better spirits, broken only by a terrifying tree stump which had Peggy dancing all over the road again. Peggy frequently shied at large rocks and tree stumps. Strange that, after so many thousands of years of domestication, horses still have that instinctive fear of the crouching predator. Nor was she too keen on the long bridge across to the island, bouncing sideways in front of the traffic and staring popeyed at the sea. She continued with caution, flicking her ears back to listen to my mindless commentary, and poised to flee if the ocean rose up to attack her.

It was three miles from the bridge to Chapeltown on the southernmost of the island's two parallel roads. After a couple of miles a man in a van stopped. "Are you Hilary?" I looked at him in astonishment. "I've been asked to show you my field. You can keep the pony there. But first you'll need to go to the hostel with your bags, so just ask for Joe at the petrol pump when you're ready." There are a lot of advantages in having an advance envoy to sort out one's lodgings.

I arrived at the Ring Lyne bar and hostel at 5.30 to an uproarious welcome. Among the revellers who spilled out of the pub to look at Peggy was a very large, very drunk man.

"Is it a horse or a mare?"

"A mare."

"I mean, is it a female animal?"

"It is."

"Are you sure?"

"Look underneath if you don't believe me."

He went ponderously over and peered between Peggy's hind legs. "'Tis a gelding."

"First gelding I've seen with teats," I said sourly, tiring of the conversation. Suddenly he was in the saddle and yelling "Giddy up!". I held the reins firmly and persuaded him that Peggy was tired and deserved a rest. He was too portly and inebriated to get his leg over the saddlebags and had to be helped down by his sniggering friends.

Finally Peggy was de-bagged and unsaddled and I trotted her bareback the mile to Joe's petrol pump and his field; eight acres of lovely lush grass. Peggy needed a proper rest, so I asked Joe if she could stay for a couple of days. She'd have company too, a donkey with hooves that had never been trimmed; they curled up like Turkish slippers.

When I arrived back at the Ring Lyne, Susanne had returned from her sightseeing full of enthusiasm for Knightstown at the far end of the island. Although our hostel had pleasant, two-bunk rooms and a large sitting room, Chapeltown wasn't exactly the hub of Valentia. Perhaps we should move on tomorrow. We ate dinner in the pub and discussed the future. Susanne had to leave Ireland in three days' time and we both, at some point, had to pick up our extra luggage from Killarney. The present stormy wet weather would continue for the next two or three days, so the forecast said, so we might as well stay another day in Valentia then hitch into Killarney and give Peggy a proper holiday.

⋃   ⋃   ⋃

We had a convivial evening in the pub and learned about the island from the publican. The inappropriately Spanish-sounding name was, it turned out, a corruption of Bheil-Inse. Oilean-Bheil-Inse means 'the island beside the flat land at the river mouth'. Islanders divided their memories into two halves: BB and AB; Before Bridge and After Bridge. The bridge was built in 1977, bringing undoubted benefits to Valentia along with an inevitable loss of island identity. Mr O'Sullivan gave us graphic descriptions of seriously ill people having to be taken by boat from Knightstown and then by rough road to hospital in Tralee. He described how horses and cattle used to cross on the same boat, or sometimes be swum across the narrow strait, and speculated on the possibility of getting Peggy across that way. It all depended on whether his son could come up with a suitable vessel. Fortunately for Peggy he didn't. "We don't see much of our young people now they can motor into Cahersiveen. They'll even go to Killarney or Tralee for a night out! I remember in the forties we had 'ballrooms of romance' where boy met girl. Everyone loved dancing in those days, but the evening would be over by 11." Before that there were country 'stages', wooden platforms by the road where people could dance.

The islanders are proud of Valentia's role in history. The island was the eastern terminus of the first transatlantic telegraph cable; the other end was in Newfoundland and the first ever telegram to North America was transmitted in 1858. Not content with this pioneering effort, the basic principles of television – translating light into its electrical counterpart (don't ask me to explain) – was discovered in 1873 by a telegrapher called Mr Hay. There must have been long boring hours when no telegrams were sent and a chap had nothing better to do than invent television.

And there's more. You can see the stone which played a part, in 1862, in the calculations of the longitude of the earth and hence the size of this planet. No, I don't understand that either, but here it is:

The Great European Arc of Longitude was measured by triangulation from this spot to a point in the Ural Mountains in Russia and certain astronomical observation were made at the two ends. From such arcs as this, measured both east and west, and north and south, the size and figures of the earth have been determined.

If you want to go further back than the 19th century, there are also some well-preserved dinosaur footprints.

We didn't find all those sights during our walk around the island, but we saw some holy ones at St Brendan's Well where roughly hewn stone crosses vied for attention with some rather charming plastic saints and virgins. The wind was so strong we had a struggle to remain upright and our walk along the cliffs above the dramatic sea was a test of balance, strength and the waterproof qualities of our clothing. On the way back I visited Peggy luxuriating in her spacious lodgings, and saw, to my annoyance, that she'd got rid of her much-hated head collar. After a search I found it, but wondered how I'd catch her when the time came.

Back in Knightstown we warmed up over tea and apple pie and got talking to a very charming, very British young man who tried to convince us that he was German. It was only when we met his mother that we conceded he was telling the truth. He had been educated at an English public school and now lived in London. The family had rented a yacht for a week but Mutti's battles with seasickness and the family rules of yachtsmanship had caused her to skip the Valentia section and go by car with Bernhard. "Why don't you stay in our hotel? And have dinner with us?" An excellent idea. They collected our luggage from Chapeltown and we moved into a damp, decaying but beautiful old hotel overlooking the harbour, which agreed to store my luggage while I popped back to Killarney for a night.

That dinner, in The Gallery Kitchen, surrounded by impressive sculptures, was one of the best I've ever had. It was run by an elegant English woman who did most of the cooking. Her artist partner sculpted during the winter and in the summer: "I nail his tiny feet to the floor and make him cook steaks which he's awfully good at." We also found exceptional singing at the pub round the corner. We were charmed by Valentia: the dramatic cliff walks above a frothing sea, the narrow lanes, congenial people, pleasant small town, and lack of popular tourist facilities.

U U U

We decided to leave separately the next morning. I wanted to head off early in order to get to the post office in Killarney, pick up my mail, post off some non-essential luggage, and be back in the hostel in time to claim a bunk. Susanne, however, had got so involved in the romance of the decaying hotel that looked out over a stormy waterfront that she chose to do a French Lieutenant's Woman act on the pier while I was ferried across to the mainland by a grumpy boatman – his only passenger.

I walked two miles to the main road carrying my plastic bag of essentials for the night and stood damply watching cars approach through curtains of rain, then whizz past ignoring my outstretched thumb. Sometimes the drivers glanced in my direction before staring resolutely ahead. I couldn't blame them for not wanting to have the interior of their car soaked by a hitchhiker of indeterminate gender. The wind blew in from the sea and there seemed no hope of a reprieve from the weather. I recalled a conversation between a farmhand and his Anglo-Irish employer after a stormy night:

"It rained thunder and lightning and lotions all night, and didn't the rain have the wheat threshed and the oats made into porridge."

"Well, you must pray for fine weather, Michael."

"What use is prayer when the wind is from the west?"

The Irishman's way with words is well known and is one of the pleasures of talking with rural people and, of course, reading Irish literature. I'd heard an erudite discussion on the subject of television. Perhaps, as one speaker suggested, the Irish are freer with their imaginative use of English because it was a language they had been forced to adopt. Or that having been a nation with no middle class they are not restrained by 'proper' English usage. Whatever the reason, when asking directions I'd rather hear 'Take the road out of town and 'tis all a fall of ground' than a more useful but less poetic British version. Information here was also agreeably coloured by the desire to please:

"How far is it to the youth hostel?"

"Three miles."

"No, make it two, Michael, the poor girl looks tired!"

Then there's the desire to impress:

"The farmyard's a dangerous place, Sir!"

"Why so?"

"When coming home last night with my gallon I met a rat. There wasn't hundreds of them, there was thousands of them. They was filing past me like sheep in the road."

"How many rats did you see, Pat?"

"Two, sir."

That same farmhand complained about his employer's dog:

"That bull bitch is a dangerous animal, Sir. Sure her bare teeth were against my naked sinews."

"Did she tear your trousers, Pat?"

"No, Sir."

The builder who eventually picked me up was concerned about Modern Youth. "I'm telling you, an educated Irishman is useless! He's soft; doesn't want to get his hands dirty!" In the good old days, he told me, there was no problem finding hard workers in the building trade "We didn't have strikes in those days." The conversation turned, as it often did, to The Troubles. "'Tis a desperate shame. It's hooligans and criminals that join the IRA." He liked England, having worked for Morris Motors in Birmingham in the fifties and he preferred to work for the 'English gentry' in Ireland. "They don't bother you. They have someone else to look after the work. The Germans, now, they're on the job the whole time watching what you do. They're that exact."

The youth hostel, when I finally arrived, was full of inexact young Germans burning sausages in the kitchen. There were no bunks left so I was allocated a mattress on the floor. Susanne, always a successful hitchhiker, had arrived before me and achieved a bed. We cooked the special goodies I'd bought in Killarney and retreated to the characterless pub down the road for a farewell drink.

Susanne left for Shannon airport early next morning.

Chapter 5

For two chilly hours I waited for a lift back to Valentia. I tried looking pathetic, cheerful and interesting in turns. I bought a newspaper but gave up reading it because I couldn't hold it and put my thumb out. I took out my book, but thought it made me look too resigned to my situation; hitchhikers need to look eager. Salvation finally came with a young German couple who not only picked me up but had no particular plan in mind and decided, without any urging from me, that Valentia would be as good a place as any to visit. I bought them a picnic lunch and we drove round the Ring of Kerry being tourists and stopping to look at trestle tables covered in 'antiques' and bric-a-brac, and photographing donkeys posing with baby goats in their pannier baskets; once again I blessed my fortune that I was not touring Ireland the conventional way. I had, of course, told the couple all about my ride and Peggy and was pleased but a little anxious when they suggested we stop at her field to say hello. I hoped she would show appropriate delight at my return but suspected she'd walk away with one of her sour looks.

To begin with, I couldn't find her. Eight acres is a lot of land, but after climbing over a couple of walls (the gateways were too muddy to use) I saw her grazing with a herd of cows. She liked cows – they were company. When

I called to her she put up her head and watched our approach carefully, then gave me that most intimate and moving of horse greetings, a whicker. To my uninitiated German friends this minimal vibrating of the nostrils was unremarkable, but I was deeply touched by such a demonstration of affection.

Most of the following morning was spent walking around the muddy fields trying to cajole Peggy into taking up her responsibilities again. She made it quite clear that she liked me as a person, but as a boss I left much to be desired. One look at my too-ingratiating smile as I walked towards her with one hand (holding the head collar) behind my back, told her that her holiday was over, and she trotted away. Eventually I went to find Joe and a bucket of horse nuts. "We could be at this all day," he said after about half an hour as Peggy galloped by with her tail in the air, shaking her head. She was interested in the contents of the bucket, but backed off whenever I lifted my hand to her neck. Eventually I managed to grab a handful of mane and she was then all sweetness and patience while Joe fetched the head collar. Trotting bareback to the hostel I could feel the tension in Peggy's muscles. She was full of beans after her rest.

While in Killarney I had given some thought about how to cure her of pulling back when tied. Enough was enough, I had to be able to leave her safely now that I was alone. I'd bought a length of foam-rubber tubing and some strong rope.

Threading the rope through the tubing, I doubled it twice round her neck, made sure the knot couldn't slip, and tied the other end to a telegraph pole. Then I retreated to watch. Sure enough, Peggy started straining at the rope but nothing could break and the padding on the rope prevented any injury. She was looking thoughtful and both the telegraph pole and her neck were intact when I came out with the bags.

The wind had changed direction, the sky was clear and the visibility marvellous after the rain. Peggy bounced across the bridge sideways, snorting and staring at the sea, then settled down to co-operate on my chosen route around Bolus Head to the youth hostel at Ballinskelligs. From the top of the hill I could see Puffin Island and the Skellig Rocks. The sky and the sea were flecked with birds. Some 20,000 pairs of gannets nest on Little Skellig and there are also puffins, guillemots, petrels and fulmars. Great Skellig, or Skellig Michael, with its monastery tantalised me further but the sea was too rough for the boat trip. Instead I sat on the hill overlooking St Finan's Bay, eating my lunch to the sound of Peggy's rhythmic grazing, and stared at the view. The Irish playwright, John Synge, wrote about this place:

> …and, over all, the wonderfully tender and searching light that is seen only in Kerry. Looking down the drop of five or six hundred feet, the height is so great that the gannets flying close over the sea look like white butterflies, and the choughs like flies fluttering behind them. One wonders in these places, why anyone is left in Dublin, or London, or Paris, when it would be better, one would think to live in a tent or hut with that magnificent sea and sky, and to breathe this wonderful air, which is like wine in one's teeth.

Peggy slithered down the steep hill to Waterville beach which was crowded with happy families. A promising green road led off the far end, which would have cut off a loop in the road had a stone wall not blocked our progress only 50 yards from my destination. It was made by a macho farmer using gigantic boulders and, after I'd hauled down a couple and dropped one on my fingers, I decided it might be easier, after all, to retrace my steps. The same cowardice persuaded me not to attempt to circle Bolus Head by linking the two dead-end tracks shown on the map with a climb across the intervening saddle. I had to readjust to being on my own again and start being more courageous but that afternoon I had the excuse that I needed to ride directly to Ballinskelligs to get to the youth hostel soon after

'A nondescript brown pony with a silly hairstyle'

Exploring Slea Head with Great Blasket Island in the background

Kathleen and Peggy

Peggy (not) swimming

Gallarus Oratory – an early Christian
chapel, the shape of an inverted boat

Dingle Harbour

Beach on Great Blasket Island, whose population was evacuated in 1953. The island produced three notable writers in the Irish language.

Cliffs near Dingle

View south from the Dingle Peninsula

Sneem, on the
Ring of Kerry

At the O'Sheas' forge

Peggy learning
to paddle at
Brandon Bay

Pony rides

Susanne sipping tea at
Kate Kearny's Cottage,
Gap of Dunloe

Macgillycuddy's Reeks

Starting the descent of Black Valley

Peggy raises her objections
to Black Valley

Bantry Bay

The lonely sheepdog on the
Knockmealdown mountains

Overlooking the
Ring of Kerry

Quatercentenary memorial
to Father James Archer who
supposedly leapt with his
horse from this point to
escape English soldiers

Wild Camping

Rock of Cashel

Stone carvings at Cashel
Cathedral

Me and Peggy on the final
day of our journey

it opened. It was a tiny hostel – only 12 beds – and I wanted to make sure I got one of them.

A warm welcome awaited us. "That's the first time we've had someone arrive this way!" said the warden approvingly, summoning a friend with a camera. "You can put the pony in with Trigger." Peggy would like this plan: she'd neighed at Trigger, a Shetland pony standing waist deep (if ponies have a waist) in purple loosestrife, as we'd approached the hostel. Trigger's child owner took us up to the field and the Shetland trotted up to greet us: an absurd equine dwarf with tiny little legs and ambivalent feelings about having a visitor for the night.

When I went to check on Peggy early next morning I found her standing companionably with Trigger in a shed; he had obviously been a good host and shown her the facilities. I felt very guilty separating the new friends, especially when both neighed frantically until out of earshot. After that, Peggy perceived every cyclist as a horse and every child's scream as a neigh. She really was exceptional in her craving for company.

When not neighing, Peggy concentrated on anticipating my route so she could be assertive about her own preferences. Every crossroads was a tussle. We were heading back to Waterville, and this time I hoped to manage the shortcut along the beach; it would be well worth it, cutting off a long stretch of main road. Peggy galloped enthusiastically to the mouth of the River Inny but refused even to consider fording it. Secretly agreeing with her that it did look wide and deep, I gave in and resigned myself to four boring extra miles.

U   U   U

Waterville was celebrating August Bank Holiday with banners across the street and a very noisy funfair which unnerved us both. It often surprised me that while I was prancing down a busy street, usually sideways if there was something upsetting Peggy, the majority of shoppers would pretend not to notice. In South America or Africa, people would have put down their baggage and relaxed into a comfortable staring posture, but in Ireland the Anglo-Saxon 'it's rude to stare' ethic is strongly adhered to. Not, I learned afterwards, that my pony and I went unnoticed. During the Mollie days I talked to someone in a pub who'd seen me a few days earlier. "She rode through the town at nine in the morning," he said to his friend. "You can imagine what that did to Lahinch! The place was buzzing for days." Yet from the amount of attention I got at the time I might as well have been invisible. People in cars feel comfortable staring, however. I'd hear the screech of brakes as they nearly collided with another ogling driver. So perhaps I left Waterville buzzing as well as blaring as we headed for Lough Currane and, I hoped, a green road over the mountains which was marked on a very old large-scale map I'd been shown in Ballinskelligs.

Maybe that road had existed once, but I could find no sign of it now. However, the wooded shores of the lake were so beautiful it was no hardship to retrace my steps and resign myself to following the main Ring of Kerry road to Caherdaniel. I'd hoped to avoid this because the prospect of riding along Ireland's most famous scenic drive in Bank Holiday traffic didn't fill me with joy. But I needn't have worried. There were plenty of cars, yes, but with long gaps in between, and it deserves its popularity. The road circles the peninsula, high up the side of the mountain, with sheer cliffs on one side, and a drop down to the sea on the other. Each curve brings a new sea view. After the rain of the last couple of days it was now clear and calm, so the sea looked Mediterranean blue and the mountains a vivid green. At Coomakesta Pass, the highest point of the drive, the road makes a hairpin bend and I found a track over the shoulder where I could be alone to take a tea break and gaze at the view that was one of the loveliest of the whole trip. I could see back towards MacGillycuddy's Reeks and the tip of the Dingle peninsula and down to a little horseshoe-shaped harbour full of yachts, their sails very white in the late afternoon sun.

I had made up my mind to camp wild that night. I'd been pretty self-indulgent recently, with hostels, B&Bs and even (gasp!) a hotel. I was missing Susanne more than I liked to admit. I had always hated asking farmers for a field for Peggy and a place for my tent. Never mind that they were usually willing and hospitable, it seemed an imposition and I was unduly sensitive to the occasional rebuff. The absolute freedom I felt when camping far from any house or road was very precious. I thought I might have found the ideal place when I followed a beautiful green road running just above the harbour. It dead-ended at a deserted house, and although it was really too early to stop, it offered such tempting camping, with a stream nearby and lovely green grass, that I had nearly made up my mind to stay. However, a peep through the window showed that it wasn't deserted after all, just apparently unoccupied. And you never know in Ireland. You see a decaying, half-ruined house and inside there's a decaying, half-ruined person.

So because of my cowardice I ended up camping by a rubbish dump. Once Peggy and I had thought of stopping for the night, we couldn't get the idea out of our heads. To Peggy's despair I passed plenty of fields with good grass, but always with a house nearby, and I just didn't want to make the effort to ask permission. So when I followed the track that turned out to be the route to the rubbish dump for Derrynane National Park and found an unfenced, overgrown field, I thought that it would do. We had gone 24 miles that day and I didn't feel like looking any further. The national park seemed to be mainly woods so we were running out of choices. And anyway, there was one big advantage to this site; a river ran past the bottom of the field beyond the wire fence, frisking over sun-warmed boulders and providing a perfect bath. I washed my clothes and hung them around on the bushes and gave Peggy a drink from my plastic bucket.

Now, I don't understand about the right sort of grass and the wrong sort of grass. To me, grass is grass, and if it's succulent and green, then it's gourmet grass. Not to Peggy, it wasn't. Maybe it was too overgrown and sour in its old age, or maybe the proximity of trees alters the flavour. I thought she would be thrilled by the ample grazing I was providing but, after I had debagged and unsaddled her, she investigated the field, ate a few mouthfuls, then came and stood by the luggage as if to say 'OK, I'm ready to go now'. While I set up the tent she paced up and down, stared at the distant horizon, then walked briskly down the grassy track leading through the woods to the 'gate' (a few strands of barbed wire) and stood hopeful of release. With hindsight I realise that she was eloquently telling me that dinner was inadequate and we should go somewhere else, but at that stage I still wasn't fluent in Peggy-speak. The only concession I made was not to tether her, though I put the hobble and chain on without attaching it to the stake. She didn't like the arrangement, but, as I explained to her, it was her own fault. I didn't want to spend another two hours trying to catch her the following morning.

I needn't have worried. I was woken at seven by Peggy strolling up and down outside the tent, clanking her chain like the Canterville Ghost. After some meandering we arrived at Derrynane House so I decided to make an unscheduled stop and learn about Daniel O'Connell who, I'm ashamed to say, I'd never even heard of until I came to Ireland. This was the man that Gladstone called 'the greatest popular leader the world has ever known' and the Irish knew as 'the Great Liberator'.

O'Connell was born in 1775 and largely brought up in Derrynane House by a rich uncle who undertook to educate the boy in France, since Catholics were denied secondary education in Ireland. He later studied law and became a successful barrister, often supporting Irish tenants in their appeals against eviction by ruthless landlords. Ireland, in those days of famine and oppression, experienced a constant seesaw of peasant rebellion followed by brutal oppression by their British overlords. O'Connell had seen enough bloodshed in the French Revolution, and declared that 'No political change whatsoever is worth the shedding of a single drop of human blood'. He set about to promote reform through legitimate channels, eventually standing for parliament (representing County Clare) in 1828 and winning by a landslide. As a Catholic he was barred from taking his seat. Such was his popular support, however, that the government, fearing civil war, passed the Catholic Relief Act in 1829. Thus O'Connell became the first Catholic Irishman to sit in parliament at Westminster where he became an advocate of Home Rule. It was while pursuing this objective that he was found guilty, in 1844, of 'creating discontent and disaffection among the Queen's subjects' and imprisoned. The House of Lords reversed the decision but during his incarceration his health deteriorated and he died in 1847 aged 72.

It has been written that 'Daniel O'Connell found the Irish peasants slaves. He left them men'. This is no exaggeration when you consider that in the late 18th century a Catholic was forbidden to purchase land, hold public office, engage in trade or commerce, enter the bar, carry a sword or own a horse worth more than £5.

From the outside, Derrynane House is an austere pair of grey rectangles, one upended and crenulated, but I found the museum inside interesting and enlightening. I was surprised to learn that this peace-loving man had killed a rival in a duel. Plagued by remorse he had thereafter worn a black glove and settled an annuity on his victim's daughter. The duelling pistols and glove are on display.

I was the only visitor, so when the nice girl at reception asked if there was anything else she could tell me I mentioned that I had a pony outside and could I possibly have permission to ride around the grounds, which I'd already discovered comprised 120 hectares of woodland and coast. Great excitement. Everyone went out to admire Peggy who was standing looking pensive, having, I think, given her padded neck rope the full test. I had a hard time undoing the knot. She never again pulled back when tied.

Derrynane House may be unimpressive architecturally but its location is nothing short of superb with its own stretch of yellow-sand beach, rocky inlets, and dunes. Alone on the beach, Peggy needed no urging into a gallop to the far end, then trotted back through the surf with her head up and ears pricked. As I patted her neck I thought proudly of how far she'd come, geographically and psychologically, from that first day in Castle Gregory when I had such doubts about her suitability for the job. I hadn't done so badly myself.

U   U   U

Caherdaniel was my next stop, specifically to visit a horse-owning publican who knew about the old road over the mountains. The green road that I'd tried to find in Waterville originally ran to Kenmare, and Ted Butler told me I should be able to pick it up at intervals along my route. He helpfully marked it on my map, but maps and reality do not always coincide. I found the section out of Caherdaniel and gave Peggy a long lunch break on some green pasture. I knew she'd been deprived the previous night. While she chomped noisily I lay back feeling the sun on my face and listening to the sounds of nature. In my drowsy state the firkins that were carried along the butter road became giant fir cones strapped to the back of Irish peasants; or perhaps they were self-propelled like one of my favourite animals, the pangolin.

One thing was certain, those firkins hadn't trotted this route for many a day. Once Peggy and I reached the top of the hill I couldn't see any sign of the path. I was feeling braver than yesterday, so rather than retracing my steps I led Peggy slowly down through very difficult terrain: bogs (though not deep), mini-cliffs, boulders and dense clumps of gorse, towards the line of houses where I judged the road to be. I was no longer terrified of bogs – just nervous;

I knew the very dry weather had rendered them much safer. Peggy never sank above her fetlocks. She was very obliging, only stopping occasionally to register her disapproval by forcing out a horse-apple. In return I was generous with her brown-bread rewards. I had to zigzag down the steep bits, retracing my steps periodically when I came to mini-cliffs. Once I was cursing her for stopping yet again, when I looked round and saw that the saddlebags had started to slip (always a problem when there was not my weight in the saddle). She was in a very awkward spot, but stood immobile until I'd undone all the straps and heaved them back into position, then pushed me with her nose and walked away. I left her to graze each time I checked the next section of the route and took down stone walls. Her longest wait was while I followed a well-worn cow path with increasing confidence as it wound its way through prickly gorse and low trees to a large field, beyond which I could see the road. When Peggy and I reached the field, however, I found we were separated from the road by a channel about five feet deep and full of water. Damn. I walked up and down it until I found a section that was less steep, with some stones providing firm footing at the bottom. Peggy courageously slid down the hill, jumped the ditch and then got into difficulties on the far bank, which was very soft mud. For an awful moment I thought she was going to get trapped in that ditch but she managed to struggle up the other side. I felt very shaken by this, but Peggy was quite calm and we were both delighted to feel tarmac beneath our feet again. I was so proud of Peggy and wished Susanne were here to join the praise. I was becoming quite soppy about her.

Peggy's delight at being on the road was short-lived since, fired with enthusiasm for butter roads, I followed an old man's advice and tried a short cut. To begin with it was a good track serving various houses, and when it dead-ended at the last house I asked directions. Despite the woman's specific instructions I went wrong and even in my new adventurous mood was so daunted by the endless expanse of bog and tussock grass that I turned back.

The kind woman caught me up, out of breath and babe in arms, to show me the proper path which, she warned me, was very rough. It was even worse than before – the three Bs, bog, boulders and bloody gorse with some very deep holes in between.

The final descent was unnervingly steep and when I got to the bottom I found that we were separated from the road by a very sturdy barbed-wire fence. Going back was unthinkable, so I examined the fence carefully and saw that the end post could be pulled up to leave a rocky and steep gap which I hoped my brave little pony could jump through (to get back on a road she'd do anything). When I pulled the post out, a stray bit of barbed wire leaped out at my face, knocking my glasses off and impaling a nostril. I could feel blood running down my upper lip and looked without success for a tissue, while pretending to adjust the saddlebags in case one of the many cars decided to stop and help. I eventually found a tissue, Peggy jumped through the gap, and I let her stay on lovely safe tarmac for the rest of the day.

U   U   U

My diary entry for 8th August reads 'Awake at 6.30 with baaing sheep and lowing of cars' which reminds me how pleasant it was to camp away from all man-made sounds as well as how my brain was decaying. Knowing that Peggy deserved a proper field that night, and having spotted a desirable-looking white farmhouse across the valley surrounded by green fields, I had struck it lucky with a sweet old man offering me a camping spot by the river. It was a perfect place, sheltered from the wind and out of sight of the farmhouse, and with acres of lovely grass for Peggy. The farmer's son came down to ask me to share a cup of tea with them just as I was enjoying a thorough wash in the river. He tactfully withdrew, but reappeared after a decent interval to ask me to come for breakfast the next morning.

My early rising enabled me to be loaded and ready to go in record time. I left Peggy to finish her breakfast and tapped tentatively on the farmhouse door. Only Dad was up; John was still sleeping, having been to a dance the night before; a major undertaking with no car. The family's last vehicle was parked in our field and occupied by some happy hens. Our conversation was halting because of my difficulty in understanding the broad Kerry accent. We talked of horses. "When I see the horse I'm remembering my father. He was the last person in this family to use a horse. Rode everywhere – Sneem, Kenmare…"

"There and back?" (Kenmare is 20 miles away.)

"There and back."

Peggy was very jaunty that morning; ears pricked so sharply I feared she'd strain them as we trotted through Sneem. This slightly self-conscious village had recently won an award for its tidiness, and was indeed very much prettier than I was accustomed to in Ireland. There was a little church with a salmon weather vane (for this is a salmon fishing area) then a bridge over the River Sneem, and a row of brightly painted houses facing the village green. And when I say brightly painted, I mean all the colours of the rainbow: purple, maroon, orange, yellow, white, pink, turquoise, green.

In Ireland, house painting seems to be the only expression of individuality left to the owners of uniformly rectangular bungalows. Even these were mostly yellow, but in terraced houses you see orange with turquoise trim, yellow and red, and the very popular chartreuse which manages not to blend with Ireland's other 39 shades of green. Sneem, however, had given some thought to colour co-ordination and was indeed a most attractive village.

I managed to pick up another stretch of butter road here. It began, as usual, as a lane serving occasional houses, the grass verges overgrown with flowers including the orange montbretia lily which has run wild in south Kerry and west Cork. Inevitably, the road ended at the last house, but while

I was debating with myself whether to turn back, a woman hobbled out to complain about Ireland. She had awful problems with arthritis, she told me. "The doctors here are rubbish, all they think about is getting their cheque from the county council… we've no proper welfare system here. In England, now, they look after their people…" And so it went on. Finally she drew herself up proudly saying, "I'm of English heritage myself." I managed to stop the flow long enough to ask if the road continued. "Yes, you'll have to open that gate. I'd do it for you but my feet, you see: when I last saw the doctor he said nothing could be done. I'll just have to live with it…"

Beyond the gate was a rocky but clearly defined track. Peggy was depressed at leaving the road but I was happy to lead her and pick blackberries which were now starting to ripen. After about half a mile we came to a gate beyond which the track joined a broad forestry road, though, irritatingly, the gateway was too narrow for Peggy plus saddlebags so I had to unload her. But at least it was unlocked and after a few miles of peaceful pine forests we emerged onto the main road and I soon saw the cheering little green 'Post' sign indicating a post office-cum-shop, along with a public phone. I needed some provisions. Dinner last night had been a creative combination of dried potato, milk powder and minestrone soup. While I was buying bread, cheese and yoghurt I spied a tourist outside taking photos of Peggy standing with her luggage underneath the 'Post' sign. I imagined the commentary back in America. "See here, isn't this quaint? They still use mail horses in the west of Ireland." The friendly shop attendant was also much taken by my means of transport. When another customer arrived he said: "I see you didn't bring your horse, Mary. 'Tis all the fashion, you know!"

A hysterical bull was bellowing hoarsely in the field outside. Since this was the beginning of the next stretch of butter road I decided to believe the fellow when he said it was blocked off. I could just as easily follow the main road for a bit. We stopped and ate lunch in a field a few miles further on. While I was musing to myself that the yarrow in these parts was the same colour as my blackberry yoghurt, a farmer arrived carrying some fearsome implement and said pleasantly that it was his bull yelling outside the post office. "I'm thinking he might make his way down here."

"Am I on your land?" I asked, anxiously.

"Yes, but you be finishing your sandwich."

We chatted about horses, bulls and the drought and he disappeared up the track, only to reappear silently just as I was having my afternoon pee.

ʊ   ʊ   ʊ

We were fast approaching Kenmare, and since I wanted to camp well before that biggish town I took my courage in both hands and turned up a rather impressive drive. A woman answered my knock. "I'm sorry to bother you, but I'm touring Ireland on horseback..." She jerked her head back and said:

"Jim, there's a tourist here with a horse." Jim peered suspiciously over her shoulder.

"Are you alone?"

"Yes."

"Quite alone?"

"Yes."

"Do you promise there's no-one else with you?"

Farmers with suitable camping fields have a hard time round the Ring of Kerry. Too many hikers, bikers and campers try to take advantage of them. Once I'd persuaded the farmer that I really wasn't concealing 13 giggling teenagers in the bushes, he was all helpfulness and showed me a good flat field with adequate fences, though he asked me to tether Peggy while I went to town. I hitched into Kenmare with ease and had a hearty and healthy meal at a wholefood restaurant. It tasted damned good – it was the first proper meal I'd had for three days. I peered longingly in the restaurant window as I rode through Kenmare the next day. Then I looked *at* the restaurant window, saw my sack-of-potatoes reflection and straightened up for one of my public appearances. Not that anyone took much notice, though the high street was busy with shoppers.

I decided to modify my original plan to follow the coastline to the end of every peninsula. Beara, I decided, would have to be explored another time. I had plotted out a route over the mountains to Bantry Bay along irresistible unsurfaced roads. I just hoped they were usable, not more blocked-off ancient green roads or tracks which petered out into bogs.

Peggy seemed depressed. When we passed a pony in a field she hardly raised a neigh. In earlier days her yells of greeting said '*Hello!* How wonderful to see you!' Now her little whinny just said 'Hi'. And she no longer bothered to greet donkeys at all. Perhaps their inferior status had been brought home to her by an unfortunate fellow who lurched towards us dragging an enormous ball and chain. Irish donkey restraints were ever ingenious. I'd seen them hobbled front legs together, back leg to front leg, and anchored to a mobile log. If Peggy was gloomy, I was uneasy. I had a feeling of foreboding about my chosen route; it was too reminiscent of Mollie's last day. Even the weather was similar, with grey clouds gathering overhead. Peggy sensed my anxiety and crawled along with the greatest reluctance, jumping at every boulder and peering wide-eyed into every gateway. I passed a stony-faced woman and child who didn't return my greeting. When I knocked on a door to ask if the road really did run over the pass, it was a ghost house, the sound echoing through the empty rooms. Grass grew up between the flagstones by the neglected garden. I rode on, thinking of the early 19th-century traveller in Kerry who was told: "Now hear me, will you sir, for it's a lonesome way you're taking, and them mountains is the place for all manner of evil doings from the living and the dead…"

We reached the last house before the road narrowed and climbed, I hoped, towards the pass. I could see someone busy in the garden, so tied Peggy to the gate and went in to make my enquiries. Several snarling dogs rushed at me as I made my way down the path to the dwarfish figure. Heavens, a double amputee... better not stare. The legless man looked up at me as he weeded his potato bed. "Sure, but you can go over the mountains. 'Tis a road all the way." He looked a bit scornful at my doubts and rose to his feet. Perhaps I should have stared after all.

Chapter 6

After the last house, the road narrowed to the width of a car, and a ribbon of grass started to appear along the middle. If I had been reassured by the gardener that the road did, indeed, run over the pass to the next valley, Peggy was still filled with foreboding. She crept along looking for things to shy at, and sulking about the steep incline. Since I had considerably done the climb on my own feet I needed a rest at the top more than she. I took out her bit and let her have a leisurely lunch while I ate my bun and apple, and took my last look at Kerry. I could see most of the county: behind me stretched the Kenmare River and its bay, and MacGillycuddy's Reeks, while ahead was the deep tree-lined river valley backed by the hills that divide Kerry from Cork.

We descended without incident into the valley. The youth hostel by the river was tempting but it was on the main road, and anyway, it was too early to stop for the night. I was still on the large-scale map and had spotted another green road over the next range of mountains to Bantry Bay. I reckoned I deserved a B&B after five nights of camping. Peggy was not impressed at this decision. She slowed to a crawl and sought out promising-looking fields that, in her opinion, would do nicely for her accommodation.

I was in no hurry to stop; it was a most heavenly valley. The narrow road that followed the east bank of the River Sheen was bordered with flowering buddleia bushes where peacocks and red admirals jostled for space, and the clumps of brambles were so covered in ripe fruit I could snatch the blackberries as I passed. It felt like early autumn. The rowan trees were red with berries and I could sniff that late summer-holiday smell of bracken, gorse and heather. The blackthorn bushes, white with flowers when I started my trek with Mollie, were now heavy with green sloes, some already turning dusky blue, and green berries clustered round the holly stems. Holly is one of the remnants of the native forests that once covered the hillsides of southwest Ireland. The holly and oak trees were mostly felled in the 17th and 18th centuries for iron smelting but a few pockets remain, especially in west Cork. This roadside greenery was striped with white from silver birch trees and masses of ripening hazel nuts dangled in easy reach above my head. I'd never seen so many; at home the squirrels would have got them. "That's it," I said aloud. "There are no squirrels here!"

I was wrong. Later research revealed that, as in England, the native red squirrel was being replaced by greys which now outnumber them six to one. It is also thought that the red squirrel became extinct there in the 17th century but was reintroduced in the early 19th. They flourished unopposed until 1911 when Lord Buckingham had the unfortunate idea of giving a dozen grey squirrels as a wedding present to the daughter of the Earl of Granard at Castleforbes, County Longford.

A wicker basket containing eight or twelve squirrels… was opened on the lawn after the wedding breakfast, whereupon the bushy-tailed creatures quickly leapt out and scampered off into the woods where they went forth and multiplied.

The ascent to the next pass was a much longer, tougher climb than the last one, and the landscape increasingly remote. And spectacular. Craggy mountains surrounded us on all sides, scooped and carved into gullies and cliffs, their green broken by patches of bracken, gorse and bog grass, while Kerry and the river valley faded into the haze behind us. Tarmac had mostly given way to gravel and grass and the feeling of being miles away from anywhere was exhilarating. When I paused to look at the map there was complete silence broken only by the distant bleating of sheep. The top of the pass was marked on the map as 'Priest's Leap', 1,895 feet, and I wondered about the origin of the name. It has a deliciously wicked ring to it – was the priest involved in an illicit liaison and leapt to his death rather than face his superiors? Or did a priest secretly go up to that place – by motorbike perhaps – and leap for the sheer fun of it?

Peggy wasn't about to do any leaping. She snailed up the steep hill with her ears back, finding every excuse she could think of to stop. I was leading her – or rather hauling her along – and got cross so took out the whip (this was normally tucked away out of sight, to be used only in emergencies) so she went to the other extreme and jogged, treading on my feet and pushing me in the back with her nose. Then she stepped on the reins and broke one of the straps that held the bit to the head collar. This made me crosser still. I tied the bit and reins to the saddlebags and went on leading her, both of us grumbling at each other, while I wondered how long it would take to reach the Glengarriff road. I could now see the inlet of sea at Bantry Bay behind another low range of hills and a patchwork of green fields. Our road, however, contoured along the side of the mountain, seemingly into infinity.

We were plodding along when I saw, to my great surprise, a car parked at the side of the road. At the same time I noticed to my dismay that I'd lost the bit and reins. Curses, I would have to tether Peggy and walk back and find them. Better make contact with the car driver first or he might think it all very strange. He'd taken his children up the pass for a picnic, and once I explained the problem he offered to drive me back to search for the missing tack while his kids looked after Peggy. A very fortuitous meeting since we found the reins on the far side of the pass – it would have taken an hour to walk back up there and down again. As we drove, Tom went straight to the point. "You single? Would you be thinking of marrying an Irish farmer, now?" He was divorced, so he said.

Reunited with our dependants, I thanked him and we went our separate ways. With that delay, and the fact that we'd been on the road for ten hours, I decided to listen to Peggy's ever more obvious hints and camp for the night. For a while we had been following a tumbling river, fed by little waterfalls, which had carved its passage deep into the valley on our right. No access there, but from time to time a small stream flowed across the road, and when I saw a patch of good grass by one of the streams and a flattish area for my tent, I stopped. The views were glorious and I could indulge myself with a B&B tomorrow. I sat outside until the sun went down, repairing the bridle and watching the red sun turn Peggy's Guinness-coloured sides to chestnut. Then as it slipped lower she became a dark silhouette outlined against the blue-green hills and glinting bay. When there was 'not enough daylight to cover the dark' I got into my sleeping bag for some cramped but cosy letter-writing by candlelight. Emerging from the tent for a final pee I found a newly risen yellow moon and the lights of Bantry and Glengarriff twinkling below. Beautiful!

I described the morning in a letter to my friend, Susie:

As I suspected, it wasn't a restful night, what with Peggy clanking her chain and blowing raspberries at me through the door and the sloping ground causing me to slide to the back of the tent. Then I was woken sharply at seven by what sounded like a full-blown cavalry charge complete with whooping Indians.

Peering out, I found myself surrounded by a large herd of sheep which were being driven up the mountain by two very efficient sheepdogs urged on by a vocal shepherd. "I hope I didn't disturb you," he said politely when he spotted me and the tent.

Peggy was still tethered and had registered her disapproval at the arrangement by depositing the biggest pile of droppings she could manage as near to the tent and my luggage as possible. I released her to catch up on the grass-that's-greener-beyond-the-tether, lit my little stove to boil water for my tea, sliced some stale brown bread which collapsed into crumbs, decided the butter really was rancid so smeared on some honey and had breakfast listening to *Today* on my radio. Such is my morning routine when camping. Then pack up the tent, picking earwigs out of the interior and slugs off the bottom, and begin the time-consuming task of fitting everything into the saddlebags. Then it's time to get Peggy but I'm always bent double by this point. Camping gives me backache and packing luggage aggravates it till I'm like a stage arthritic. I manage to straighten up by the time I'm ready to load her, which is a good thing since I need all my height, and strength to heave the saddlebags into position. This is where Peggy's experience in harness really pays off – she stands stock-still as she's been taught to do while the harness is put on. The whole process from getting up to getting on takes at least 1½ hours. I suppose it's progress from the 2½ hours when I first started this trip.

We were nearer civilisation than I'd realised, and before long we joined a proper road that closely followed the very lovely River Coomhola whose dark mysterious waters slid past huge moss-covered boulders overhung by trees. At the main road I had to make a decision – should I turn right to Glengarriff or left to Bantry? Either would have a selection of B&Bs. I went left and had only gone a few yards when a car stopped and the driver came toward me saying, "We were just talking about you!" It was a couple from

Marlow (three miles from my home) giving a lift to the German mother and son with whom Susanne and I had dined in Valentia. Having rejoined their hired yacht, they were hitching back to the island to pick up their car. Such a happy coincidence couldn't be ignored so it didn't take long for Bernhard and his mother to convince me to make this a rest day and join them and the rest of the family for dinner on the yacht that evening. So in a few miles, to Peggy's surprise and delight, we turned into a 'Farmhouse Accommodation' drive where our night-time requirements would be taken care of.

ʊ ʊ ʊ

I had letters to post and mail to pick up in Glengarriff and quickly got a lift with a local man who knew the legend of the Priest's Leap. It was in 1612, he told me, when Father James Archer, fleeing from English soldiers, leapt with his horse from the top of the pass and landed just outside Bantry – a distance, as the horse flies, of at least ten miles. He told me there was a monument at the place where he landed showing the imprint of his horse's shoe. I never found this, but retracing the route recently I found a quatercentenary monument (a carved stone) marking the spot on the top of the pass, along with a metal cross.

This was my first mail pickup since arriving in Dingle three weeks ago, and I'd been anticipating it with increasing enthusiasm. In those days, with no mobile phones and very few call boxes, a traveller in Ireland was completely isolated. This was part of the pleasure but also added a touch of anxiety. This wasn't the place or time to receive bad news.

"How did you say you spelt your name?" The girl in the Glengarriff post office shuffled through the letters sitting in the B pigeonhole of the poste restante shelves and handed me a satisfyingly large number of envelopes. I retreated to a nearby café to read them and had one of my prosopagnosia moments. You don't know what this means? Nor did I at that time, I just knew that I had a problem recognising people. A shirtless man was sitting at a table as I came in and shouted, "Hey, hello, come over here!" So I said, "Hello!" in equal delight thinking him to be the farmer who had helped to retrieve Peggy's reins the previous day. So I bought him a cup of tea and was ever so chatty until the truth slowly dawned that he was not my farmer at all but one of the ferrymen touting for custom to take trippers to the nearby Garinish Island.

Glengarriff didn't impress me. There were coach-loads of tourists, every other house seemed to be a B&B or hotel, and when I finally found somewhere to get a bite to eat (I'd left the café in a hurry) I was served lumpy packet soup and plastic cheese between two slices of Wonderloaf by a surly girl who charged me more than I'd paid for a full meal in other places. This is what I wrote back in 1984, but having returned recently I must admit to having done Glengarriff an injustice. The row of multicoloured houses (and, yes, hotels and B&Bs) which make up its main street are varied in architecture, and sit in a deep glen backed by craggy mountains. With its location around an inlet at the head of Bantry Bay, it deserves its large number of visitors.

The name Bantry Bay had a familiar ring about it. I'm not sure if I actually remember the attempted French invasions from school history or whether I was confusing it with Botany Bay, but reading up about it provided me with further understanding of the Irish struggle for independence. This time it was the strangely named Wolfe Tone who was the local hero. Unlike the Catholic Daniel O'Connell, born 12 years later, Tone was born into a Protestant family in 1763. He also studied law, practising as a barrister in London where he found Whig allies to the cause of Home Rule in Ireland. With the French Revolution in full spate, rebellion was very much in the news. Even among liberal Whigs, however, there was little support for a break with Westminster, whilst Tone wanted an Irish parliament as well as full religious emancipation. To this end he founded the Society of the United

Irishmen in 1791 and, abandoning hope of parliamentary reform, sought the help of France to achieve his aims through force of arms. Although not yet officially at war with Britain, Napoleon Bonaparte's France was happy to join forces against its traditional foe.

The French fleet that arrived in Bantry Bay in 1796 was impressive: 43 ships and over 14,000 men. With five per cent of the Irish population now members of the United Irishmen, it was reasonable to suppose that they would rise up against the British in support of the invaders. As it was, the December weather was against the French and after waiting several days for the gales to abate so they could make a landing, they returned to France – much to Wolfe Tone's disgust: 'We were close enough to toss a biscuit ashore.' Had it been a calm day, Irish history might have been very different.

After further attempts to generate an uprising with the help of the French, Wolfe Tone was captured and sentenced to death in 1798; he committed suicide before the hangman could carry out his duty. He is remembered for his attempt to unite the people of three religions, Protestants, Catholics and Presbyterians ('Dissenters') into one cohesive group of Irishmen, a necessary first step to achieving Home Rule:

> To subvert the tyranny of our execrable government, to break the connection with England, the never failing source of all our political evils, and to assert the independence of my country – these were my objects. To unite the whole people of Ireland, to abolish the memory of all past dissentions, and to substitute the common name of Irishman, in the place of the denominations of Protestant, Catholic, and Dissenter – these were my means.

Bantry House owes its opulence to the failed French invasion. Its owner, Richard White, trained a militia to oppose the landing, and provided storage in Bantry House for munitions. He was awarded his baronetcy 'in recognition of his spirited conduct and important services' at that time and later became the first Earl of Bantry. The White family had every reason to be grateful for the turmoil in France – his son, the second earl, filled Bantry House with some very choice pieces of French furniture which were going for a song at the time. It is the stateliest of Irish stately homes, jaw-droppingly beautiful inside and with a formal garden and a hundred acres of woodland. Without Peggy to worry about, I could indulge in a proper visit and stroll around the grounds while filling up the time before I was due to meet the Schünemanns. Bernhard had suggested that I intercept his father and young friend (who weren't expecting me) as they docked the yacht at 6 o'clock, to be joined later by Bernhard and Margret.

A keen wind nagged me as I paced up and down the pier and watched fishermen unloading boxes of mussels. I saw no fish being landed, but many years ago a traveller (or maybe a Bantryman) had written that 'you could fall off the pier and they [the fish] would support your back'.

The Germans were embarrassed to find a lone woman watching their every move as they brought the boat in and tied up. They said afterwards that they assumed I was a highly critical expert. Bernhard and his mother arrived later than expected; they had not had an easy time getting lifts. "I have to teach Mother to be a better hitchhiker," said Bernhard. "She doesn't understand the proper etiquette. Like you can't turn down the radio or open windows or say 'in Germany it is other' when people talk about forestry practices." Margret took the teasing in great good humour and I was delighted to be sharing a meal with friends again, even such new ones.

ʊ   ʊ   ʊ

It was a grey morning when I left my rather pricey B&B. I'd been thoroughly spoiled by the non-commercial hospitality of most Irish farmers, so to be charged two Irish pounds for Peggy's accommodation shook me. Peggy would have told me it wasn't worth the price. She was standing waiting for me at the gate and neighed her greeting. This was not affection: she'd kicked over her bucket of water and raised a thirst, and had evidently been trying to explain her plight to a neighbouring farmer. "Whose pony is that?" he asked eyeing me suspiciously. "Who gave you permission to put it in this field?" Farmers were always on the lookout for tinkers who turn their horses into any field that happens to be handy.

My plans after Bantry were completely fluid. I had no idea where to go next so, while waiting for the Germans, had called in on the tourist office for their advice. The girl suggested a circuit round Sheep's Head, a long finger pointing into the sea which had only beauty to commend it so was seldom visited by tourists. That suited me fine. Soon I had to head inland to make my way to County Waterford where a friend was expecting me, and such a narrow peninsula would help satiate me with the ocean. But it was a grey sea I rode beside; a grey sea under a grey sky skulking low over the hills. A few gloomy cormorants were drying their wings on rocks, while I had my picnic overlooking the bay. Then in the afternoon the sun came out and transformed the colours to those of a child's painting: blue sky, green hills, yellow gorse, turquoise sea. Later, as we progressed along the narrow road known as the Goat's Path, the sea turned silver and the mountains of Kerry stood in dove-grey rows across the bay under a wallpaper-cream sky.

Peggy indicated that she was thirsty and since I could find no running water I knocked at a door. Three little red-haired children ran out in great excitement and were lifted into the saddle by Dad while Peggy drank long and deep from a blue washing-up bowl.

Fingers of cloud were tickling the surface of the ocean. With a sea mist on its way I hesitated briefly before deciding to continue to the end of the peninsula. It was easy to be seduced by the scenery – the changing sea and sky, lumpy hills and stunted vegetation: wind-sculpted trees, heather and bracken.

Sheltered hollows protected tall trees and houses and by 7 o'clock I could no longer ignore Peggy's hints that it was time to stop for the night. I rode up the drive of a beautiful farm surrounded by green fields and said my piece to a startled-looking mother and son. No, they hadn't got any available field. Peggy was even more disgusted at this obvious lie than I was, and almost refused to leave. Actually I could well understand their desire to reserve their best pasture in time of drought. I thought perhaps I could camp wild but could find no running water. Then a loose horse trotted up and my heart sank; I'd never get rid of it. I implored Peggy not to neigh and amazingly she held her peace, and when I brandished my whip the visitor lost interest and wandered away.

The wild part of the peninsula ended as I crossed the neck of the mountains and started down towards the more populated, sheltered southern road. An old man standing by his gate peered at me. "Is that a mule?" He still kept a workhorse, he told me, but was unsympathetic to my plight. "No, I've no land." Could he suggest somewhere? "No. It's still early, you can go on someways." I went on 100 yards or so and finally met with success. A young farmer milking his cows had no objection to my camping in one of his fields and showed me where to put the tent. As I was leading Peggy through the gate I heard a shout. The old man was standing silhouetted against the sky waving his arms negatively. To my acute embarrassment I realised they were father and son. Whatever Dad's objections had been, the young man brushed them aside and the old man came into the field all friendly for a chat and brought me some milk.

One of my fibre-glass tent poles had broken. The tent could still be pitched but its rear end didn't look right. Mine didn't feel right either after 21 miles. I sat down carefully outside the tent, sipping my milky coffee and watching a cheese-coloured moon rise over the evening clouds. Peggy was lying down. Rest for the weary travellers.

We did another 20 miles the next day, heading back east along the southern road, but my memory is of a sun-drenched stroll by the sea with languid curlews wandering along the shore and a heron flapping lazily overhead. When the road veered inland, baby rabbits dithered by the roadside, and a prurient pair of donkeys, distracted from their business by the sight of Peggy, followed along their side of the fence *in flagrante.* The bushes were heavy with blackberries. Frustrated by my hit-or-miss passing grabs, I dismounted and filled a plastic bag which I tied in front of the saddle. Then, spurred out of my lethargy by the thought of a blackberry lunch, I urged Peggy into a trot. Result: blackberry sludge. I dumped it, and Peggy, who like all animals hated to see food wasted, ate the sludge so her granny lips were covered in purple froth. Thereafter I had to compete with her in blackberry picking. She became quite skilful, plucking them delicately off the stem one by one.

It was Sunday. I passed a couple of villages with clusters of people gossiping outside the church, but otherwise the road was deserted. At Friendly Cove I took my last look at the sea which I had now followed, on and off, for over 700 miles, and headed east.

Chapter 7

At Durrus I headed inland towards Dunmanway and a tilled landscape of patchwork fields. Almost immediately the atmosphere changed. The air felt softer without the sea breeze, and smelt of grass and cows instead of seaweed and bracken. I followed a river known as Four Mile Water, and while giving Peggy a long tea break on the juicy grass verge, I spied some promising white blobs in a cow pasture. Mushrooms! I collected far too many and, tying the bag carefully to the saddle, I continued to a farm, set in such improbably green fields they couldn't possibly say no to my camping request. The Crawleys wouldn't have said no if they lived in a desert. The lounge, where I sat with the family and their friends drinking tea and watching the Olympics on TV, radiated warmth, humour and friendship. A beautiful boy of about 18 stared at me with large brown eyes. "He's brain damaged, poor lad," explained the farmer. "Can't speak." Peggy had acres and acres of mushrooms to trample. I could hardly bear it; I already had far too many. Supper was mushroom soup followed by fried mushrooms on bread, with mushroom salad on the side.

I heard no Peggy sounds during the night and got up to look for her in some anxiety the next morning. She had five interconnected fields to choose from so of course I found her in the farthest one, lying down in the dewy mushroomy grass. During my search I'd made the unwelcome discovery that I was sharing the acreage with a large virile-looking bull as well as cows. I hoped the bull wouldn't get it into his head to show off to the ladies. They all crowded round to watch me pack up the tent, the steam rising from their lowered heads. I tried to avoid making any sudden movements; my Waterford friend had recently been tossed by a bull, cracking a vertebra, so I was doubly cautious. And frightened.

During this slow-motion performance Peggy had got bored and strolled over to the gate in the hope of finding someone more competent than me. Then, as I was pulling up the zip on the saddlebag, she sauntered back with a resigned expression and waited to be saddled. The bull and cows followed me to the gate with what I hoped was friendly curiosity and allowed me to leave with my vertebrae intact.

My choice of route was excellent; a narrow track took me over some very wild, rock-covered hills, bright with flowering heather, and down into a valley where the tower house of Castle Donovan dominated the scene. Built in 1560 by Donal O'Donovan, it was damaged by Oliver Cromwell's troops and is now gently crumbling into the landscape. "You've got a grand rigout there," called out an old man on a bicycle as I trotted past. I was heading for an independent hostel that had been recommended by one of my dorm-mates in Valentia.

υ υ υ

Dunmanway is not on any tourist route so the newly opened Shiplake hostel was half empty. It was a very special place, my favourite of all the hostels I stayed at, run by Mel and Vary Knivett, an English couple practising The Good Life. West Cork seemed particularly favoured for organic smallholdings, and I met several English and German families working the land. The Knivetts grew their own organic vegetables and made and sold dairy products with the help of the sweet-faced Jersey cow called Hazel. I liked Shiplake and its produce (especially the yoghurt and ice cream) so much that I decided it was time Peggy had a rest day and I went into Cork to collect my next batch of mail and buy a battery for my inoperable camera. There was only one other family staying in the hostel so I had the dormitory to myself, and after the Germans had finished cooking vegetarian spaghetti in the kitchen I could pick the caterpillars out of my organically grown cabbage and prepare my own cholesterol-rich meal. Mel himself had done all the renovating of what was once a derelict cottage, and had done a beautiful job. The bunks were comfortable, the loo – a long-drop above a grassy bank – serviceable, and the shower, open to the sky with steam-loving plants growing from cracks in the wall, delightful. Peggy was equally happy in her field with Hazel for company.

I should add at this point that since then Shiplake has been upgraded to become one of the most highly-praised independent hostels in Ireland, so you no longer have to traipse out into the night for a pee.

One of the Knivetts' English farmer friends was going to Cork the following day to get some cheese-starter, so I was able to cadge a lift. Having arranged to meet Paul at the creamery, I arrived in good time and watched the milk churns brought in by every possible means of transport – lorry, tractor, saloon car, donkey cart, pony cart. The milk was weighed and a chit signed. Paul turned up with his churns in the back of the car and soon we were driving along the little lanes towards Cork and talking about the joys and sorrows of self-sufficiency in Ireland. Lovely in the summer but hell in the winter (at least for a man living alone). I heard how one year Paul and his friends had scythed, threshed and winnowed the wheat by hand. "It was quite enjoyable but damned hard work and there was the constant anxiety of the weather breaking. Now I hire a combine harvester: a wonderful machine!"

We arranged a meeting time and place and I set out to see a bit of Cork and do my shopping. First, I picked up my mail; this was a mistake since the news I read dulled any desire for sightseeing. Captain Flint, the African grey parrot who'd lived with my family for 30 years, was dead. He'd been ill when I left England so I thought I was well prepared for his death but I wasn't. I walked through Cork with tears running incontinently down my face. I still miss him. It's worth a little diversion to talk about Flint; there are not many pets that are with you for three decades. He was born in the Gold Coast (now Ghana), purchased as a chick by a colleague of my father who was working in West Africa at the time. I was 12 when my mother drove us, grumbling children, to Waterloo to pick up 'a crate' that had been shipped from Africa. We stayed in the car reading until we heard shouts and laughter on the platform. Coming towards us was a porter swinging a large home-made cage. Inside was Captain Flint with his head thrust through the bars. He and the porter were competing as to who could whistle the loudest.

Flint was only shut in his cage at night. He had a perch outside the upper window and one on top of his cage. He used the increasingly tattered curtain as a ladder from one to the other, taking time out to swing wildly from the pelmet. However cold it was, the window had to be open in the morning so he could greet the milkman. Flint recognised the milk float long before we could see it, and hastened up the curtain to welcome the milkman with his whistles. His greeting was always returned. The dustmen produced the opposite effect. When he saw them coming he hurried down to the windowsill and wrapped himself in the curtain where he stayed motionless, with just his red tail showing, until the danger was over. He nearly had a nervous breakdown when milkman and dustmen arrived together.

Flint was a poor linguist. Despite our efforts he only learned one phrase – and that was one we accidentally taught him because he was always getting up to mischief. "What *are* you doing?" he would ask at intervals. He did do a perfect Greenwich Time Signal, however, and even now, when I hear the pips, I think of him.

U   U   U

There's a saddler in Cork so I bought Peggy a tasteful new lead rope and some Extra-tail fly-spray. Now we were inland, away from the sea breeze, I couldn't bear to see her so tortured by insects; she would just have to get accustomed to aerosol sprays, just as she'd finally accepted being tied. Her unsuccessful struggle against the rope that secured her by Derrynane House had done the trick. Poor Peggy, it was ironic that her fight against servitude to the English was extinguished outside the house of Daniel O'Connell.

There was a new arrival at the hostel. A very blonde, very young, very shy, very pink German with a bicycle. "I thought in Ireland there is many rain. But there is many sun!" After a teatime snack of full-cream milk, brown bread spread with cream and topped with bramble jelly, and ice cream, I went to saddle Peggy and give promised pony rides to the family before having a luggage-free canter. Then I found a very strong tree, tied Peggy round the neck with the padded rope, and gradually taught her, with the help of the Knivetts' best organic bread, that the aerosol spray was not going to kill her. She hated it to the end, but did learn not to struggle when I produced it.

After Shiplake I planned to follow as straight a line as possible to Blarney. I couldn't quite bring myself to avoid this famous attraction although I had no intention of kissing the Blarney Stone. After that I would take as scenic a route as possible across the southern part of Ireland to Lismore, County Waterford, to stay with my travel-writer friend Dervla Murphy. My odyssey thus became a journey. Now, when plotting the next part of the route, instead of my eye settling on the brown and blue bits of the map that indicated mountains and river valleys, and picking out the promising dotted lines of footpaths and tracks, I became, as they say, goal orientated.

Fortunately, serendipity is never far away in Ireland. Soon after settling down to lunch by a stream which offered a free supply of watercress to go with my cheese sandwich, I saw movement out of the corner of my eye. It was an otter. It came strolling along the mud and stones at the edge of the river, sniffing the air in a short-sighted sort of way, its dark coat in wet spikes and its blonde whiskers quivering. I tried to creep closer but it heard my approach and splashed hurriedly away.

A nearer goal than Blarney was the Kinneigh round tower which, I had read, was unique in that it is the only one built on a hexagonal base. During my travels with Mollie I had spotted the remains of round towers in Galway and Clare standing enigmatically on the skyline, but had never investigated them, although round towers are a speciality of Ireland. They were always attached to monasteries and most were built in the days of the Viking invasions, so dated from before the first millennium. No one can agree on their purpose. Certainly they were religious buildings, built by highly skilled monks, so may have simply been created for the glory of God, a finger pointing to heaven, and as bell towers (the Irish name *cloigtheach* means bell house). The four openings, or windows, at the top were usually aligned with the cardinal points of the compass, which would have had religious significance. Perhaps they were also safe-deposit places for monastic treasures. Some think they were used as places of refuge, which is why the door is generally not at ground level, so accessible only by rope ladder which could be hastily drawn up. Round towers would seem particularly uncomfortable hiding places, though. I imagined a brown spiral of monks sitting on the central staircase with the rope ladder coiled at their feet, waiting for the 'all clear'. Actually, looking at Kinneigh pointing insolently at the sky next to its church I was reminded of a remote tribe of Indians I once visited in Bolivia. They too had a church and a separate bell tower, built by the missionaries, but they worshipped the tower as a phallic symbol and sacrificed animals in front of it.

U U U

"I wonder if you can let me have a field for my tent and my pony for the night?"

"That I can. And you come in now for a cup of tea." I was served tea in the sitting room where the TV, full of sound and fury, but pictureless, was the only secular decoration. There were seven religious paintings, along with china decorated with religious motifs and two statuettes of Jesus and Mary lit by a candle. "Sorry I haven't any white bread," said Mum as she brought me freshly baked 'brack' (brown bread), ham and tomatoes.

I was woken at 6 by a scraping noise. Peggy was scratching her back on a low-hanging branch with a look of ecstasy on her face. She ignored my greeting so, rebuffed, I went back to sleep. I was just boiling my water for breakfast when I was summoned to the house for 'a cup of tea'. I was no longer surprised, but no less delighted, when this turned out to be a full breakfast. I still marvel at the generosity of the Irish. Before saddling up I gave Peggy another back scratch, her favourite on the side of her withers. It made her mouth quiver like a dowager who's been told an off-colour joke, which always made me smile.

The rocky sheep pasture of coastal Cork had given way to wheat fields enclosed by hedges and the record harvest had brought a new bonus: spilt grain on the road. The radio warned drivers to take care, 'it's as dangerous as black ice', but next day I collected bagfuls for Peggy who kept her eyes peeled for the telltale golden splashes. I let her pause and hoover up the grain. "That's an economical way of travelling! Just needs an occasional change of water I see!" said a cyclist cheerily as he splashed through the smelly evidence while I struggled up from the river with a bucket. A car passed full of waving black-and-white figures, and a mile or so later one of the nuns ran out of a house and invited me in for tea. Peggy was thrilled: they were horse breeders and had loose boxes full of elegant animals. Not for riding, of course – no-one seemed to ride for pleasure in Ireland – but for showing in hand. There were other stables along our route. By the time we wearily reached a B&B near Blarney after a 21-mile day, Peggy's throat must have been sore from neighing. It was my favourite accommodation of the trip. Four laughing daughters greeted me delightedly and escorted Peggy to a rather threadbare field full of young calves which followed her around hopefully, looking for an udder.

Next morning, Mr O'Keefe drew me a careful map showing a short cut to the castle entrance. I don't quite know how I ended up in the castle grounds, but, after apologising for trespassing to a rather frightening woman on a bicycle, I found that the exit I was planning to slip through surreptitiously had a cattle grid and a narrow gate. There's no way you can surreptitiously unload and reload a nervous pony. Peggy was no better on private land than I am; she too hated trespassing.

Blarney is famous for the wrong reason, but this doesn't matter if the lure of kissing the stone draws more visitors than would normally be attracted to a very fine castle set in splendid grounds. The view from the top, of the 'Big House' set in formal gardens planted with beech, chestnut and cedar, is magnificent. Visitors who don't have an anxious pony tied up outside can spend some happy hours exploring the 60 acres of varied parkland, including a poison garden. If you've ever wondered what wolf's bane or mandrake look like, here you are. Paul from Shiplake, who had built his own home, had told me how much he admired the castle's 15th-century builders for its clean lines and carefully calculated strength: the walls are 12 feet thick at the base but then taper upwards. The Blarney Stone is under the battlements above an 80ft drop. Whoever thought up the idea that the gift of eloquence would only be bestowed if the kisser bent backwards to do his or her obsequious act had a shrewd eye on the commercial – not to mention erotic – possibilities. A strong and eloquent Irishman is required to ensure that tourists don't plunge to their deaths (though not even a doll could actually fit through the gap beside the stone) and the official photographer is the only one who may record the scene. To add to the excitement, a conspicuous sign near the stone gives the location of the nearest defibrillator. The origin of the kissing tradition is obscure, but the story goes that Queen Elizabeth I put considerable effort into trying to wean the Lord Blarney off 'dangerous Irish practices' (the mind boggles). When he countered with 'fair words and soft speech' – she expostulated, 'This is all Blarney. What he says he never means!'.

U U U

I headed north towards the Blackwater River which runs from the hills of Kerry, through Lismore, to Waterford. I loved the inland scenery of little green fields bordered by unruly hedges or bracken-covered banks brightened by clumps of gorse, but had to admit to myself that the inland scenery is not as varied as the coast where the views and light are constantly changing. So it was on the quiet lanes of Co Cork that I first realised that I could read on horseback. A marvellous discovery, since I'd come to a particularly enjoyable bit in my book, *Good Behaviour* by Molly Keane. To give my thighs a rest I sometimes read sitting sideways in the saddle. The Pony Club would be horrified.

A fine rain was falling in the late afternoon when I came to a deep wooded valley. Ahead of me were the Nagle Mountains; they looked gentle enough on the map – none of the closely crowded contours or dark browns that are so exciting to the adventurous map reader – but they still commanded respect so I decided to stop early for the night. Crossing a bridge over a river, I saw below me a grassy clearing in the pine forest with a newly constructed path leading to it. By the little silver gate was a sign announcing that this was a Mass rock. I went to have a look. Beyond the grassy clearing a narrow footbridge crossed the stream and the path led to the rock were Mass was celebrated in Penal times (the 17th and 18th centuries when Catholics were forbidden to practise their religion). Asimple aluminium cross marked the rock, along with a plaque in Irish and English.

It was a perfect campsite. It had fresh running water, flat ground for the tent, and plenty of lovely green grass. I had to unload Peggy on the road and coax her up the flight of steps, through the narrow gate and down 12 steps to the clearing. There was no need to tether her in such an enclosed area, I just stretched her rope across the entrance to the path to discourage her from gazing over the gate and drawing attention to herself.

I still hadn't learned about The Wrong Sort of Grass, nor did I correctly interpret Peggy's strange behaviour that evening. Instead of settling down to graze, she showed an uncharacteristic interest in my activities. She hung around the campsite putting her nose into everything, chewing the tent and my jacket, and showing particular interest in my soup cooking on the stove. I was afraid she'd burn herself (or knock over the soup) so pushed her away. Undeterred, she came back and I found her standing with a guy rope in her mouth dangling its tent peg. Of course it was all very endearing and I didn't really have the heart to get cross. I even let her lick out my saucepan.

Next morning I was woken at 6.00am by Peggy stamping and snorting around the tent. My little room wobbled as she tripped over guy ropes and rubbed her chin along the flysheet. "For heaven's sake go *away*!" I shouted. She did. I dozed in blessed silence for another hour and then unzipped the flap and looked out. I couldn't see her. She must be behind the tent near the river. I dressed, crawled out and looked around in increasing disbelief. Peggy had gone. A wave of sheer panic swept over me as I recalled that morning in the mountains of the Dingle Peninsula when I first realised that Mollie was missing. Struggling to keep calm I considered the possibilities. Had she been stolen? It was possible, but unlikely in such a hidden spot and with my tent close by. I checked the area for hoof prints but the ground was too hard to see them. With her fear of bridges I was sure she wouldn't cross the narrow footbridge to the shrine. Then I noticed that the ground had been disturbed around the path leading to the gate; it looked as though she'd scrambled up the bank to get round the rope blocking her exit. There were definitely fresh prints on the path which was strewn with wood chippings; I'd smoothed it last night after pitching the tent to cover up the evidence of our visit. The gate was closed but she'd either jumped down onto the road or climbed up an equally steep bank through the pine trees to a large field above. I pulled myself up the bank to the field, praying that she'd be there. She wasn't.

I tried to think calmly. Before Mollie's death I might not have been too worried, but now I'd learned what horrible surprises can lie in wait for the unprepared; I was beside myself with anxiety. Suppose she was hit by a car? Or hurt in a dozen other ways? I thought she would probably head back to the stables where she'd enjoyed such good hospitality the day before, so started back along the road. It curved between high banks and I could never see more than 100 yards ahead of me. This was ridiculous; I'd never find her this way. Perhaps I should flag down a passing car? But there was no traffic on this minor road and she'd had over an hour's head start. I returned to the campsite to collect my binoculars and on impulse crossed the footbridge and said a little prayer at the shrine. Then I climbed back to the field above the gate where I could get a good view over the surrounding countryside. A herd of cows was grazing in a field about half a mile away. And among the black-and-white animals was a brown one. Could it be…? I jogged across the upper field to the bramble-covered bank that bordered the cow pasture and climbed up. There were the cows, and among the Friesians was one brown Hereford. I was bitterly disappointed. Of course I should have realised that Peggy couldn't just join a herd of cows in an enclosed field. But then I saw her; she was standing by the fence watching me out of the corner of her eye as she stuffed herself with grass. Then she walked towards me with a little whicker.

Just how or why Peggy came to be in that field I'll never know. The gate was open so she probably just walked in looking, as always, for company. But how did she find a field so far off the road she knew? If, as seemed equally possible, someone had come across her in the early morning and kindly put her in with the cows, why hadn't he shut the gate? I couldn't imagine who would be up at that hour anyway. Thinking the occupants of the house opposite the field might be my saviours, I knocked gently on the door to proffer my thanks. But the house was still asleep.

Adhering to the rule that gates should be left as you find them, I led Peggy out and of course was followed by a herd of cows. Perhaps on normal days they obligingly take themselves into the farmyard for milking, but today they all accompanied me down to the road while I ineffectually said, "Shoo". I had just tied up Peggy and collected a long stick to drive them back when the flustered farmer appeared on the scene. "I think I may owe you a big thankyou," I said between moos, but he just looked mystified when I explained about Peggy.

Each time I tied Peggy that day she whinnied when I returned. "Bitch!" I said.

"Think I'll forgive you that easily?" It was a blustery day; the grey sky above the forestry pines were full of wind-blown crows as we climbed the heathery hill to the pass over the Nagle Mountains and dropped down through beech and holly to the Blackwater Valley. Just before the main road I passed a house with a B&B sign, a row of beehives and a 'honey for sale' notice. Mmm, honey! I tied Peggy to a gate and went in. Two women came towards me: they were mother and daughter and mother's left eye had disappeared beneath an enormous swelling. She was allergic to bee stings and had been stung on the eyelid a few hours earlier. She hastened to add that they were her husband's bees and he didn't even notice the stings. Yes, they could sell me some honey and how about a cup of tea? The daughter went out to offer words of comfort to Peggy while I gratefully munched on fruitcake and drank numerous cups of tea (my breakfast had understandably been a bit inadequate) and chatted about bees and England. I wasn't allowed to pay for the jar of honey I took away with me.

If I had been unnerved by Peggy's adventure, she was transformed. Thereafter, I couldn't leave her for more than a few minutes before I would hear her neigh, and have to go out to reassure her that I still loved her, and promise that I would never tell her to go away again. Endearing though this was, it did put a dampener on some of my pleasures. She had always had a puritan streak and disapproved of pubs, but now it was like being back in the days of prohibition. I would just be settling down to my glass of Guinness when I'd hear pitiful neighs and have to finish my drink by her side. She didn't even have the excuse that she was tied up so couldn't share the refreshment. One time when I was enjoying a drink in the evening, knowing she was safe in an adjoining field next to my tent, I was called back by heart-rending sobs. I mean neighs. This time I thought she must be greeting another horse nearby, but no, she wanted me. So I had to forgo a second glass of Guinness and return to the tent and write my diary by candlelight.

U   U   U

I could have followed the River Blackwater to Lismore but that would have been along the main road. Besides, I wanted to visit friends of the Knivetts, organic-farming enthusiasts in Shanballymore, not far from Mallow. The map showed a track crossing the river at an encouragingly marked 'ford', but the boreen I took ended in a farm, not the river, and I was too cowardly to knock on the door and ask. I'd been horse-travelling for over two months now and had rarely met anything but kindness and hospitality from farmers; that my shyness should so irrationally persist infuriated me. I ended up adding another four or so miles to the day's total and was so irritated by my shortcomings I could hardly enjoy the views of the magnificent Blackwater with its deep wooded banks. Eventually, crossing by the Ballyhooly bridge, I was cheered by the impressive view of the castle overlooking the broad, gently flowing river. Before the bridge there was a ford here, and the castle was built in the 16th century as a defence against enemy incursions (the river otherwise providing an effective barrier).

The lanes leading to Shanballymore were peaceful, narrow and fly-ridden. I found an adequate picnic spot by the roadside and sprayed Peggy – much to her anguish – with Extra-tail. At least I had the sense not to tie her up while I did it, and to reward her with her favourite brown bread afterwards. Peggy was hungry after her adventurous night so, deciding to give her an extra-long lunch break, I settled down with my book. I soon became aware of someone clearing his throat. "Do you mind parking the horse a bit further down? There's a man here going to throw a bowl." I gave him one of my blank looks and he pointed down the road, and sure enough there was a man, surrounded by onlookers, about to throw a metal ball down the road. And when I was out of the way he threw it; someone marked the spot it landed with chalk, and they continued on their way. Afterwards I read up about road bowling, a Cork tradition (they held the first World Championship the following year). The bowl is a cast-iron cannonball which, in the right hands, or hand, can achieve speeds of 165mph and a distance of 200 yards. The technique looked, to me, a bit like cricket, but is bowled underarm. The team that completes the agreed stretch of road in the fewest number of throws is the winner.

U U U

The Wenlocks and their organic-farming methods were well known, so I was able to get directions to their smallholding. After pitching my tent near the cabbages and tethering Peggy on the lawn, I drank goat's milk and talked with Chuck and Gilly about their efforts to keep at least one of the Irish county crafts alive. Two elderly brothers in the Waterford town of Tallow made willow baskets, a craft they learned from their father. When they retire there will be no-one to continue the tradition, so Chuck went there each week to learn the craft. Bundles of willow, some white and some brown, were hanging in the shed. The Wenlocks cut their own white willow but the brown (which is artificially coloured) had to be imported at great expense from England. The native Irish willow is weaker and shorter.

When I was staying at Lismore I visited Tallow and the two old basket-makers. One of the brothers showed me a baby's cradle that a man had brought in for repair. It had been his cradle when he was an infant, and now he wanted it for his firstborn. The old man remembered making it.

I had the uncomfortable feeling that, in terms of dominance, Peggy now had the upper hand. First her pathetic neighs were far more effective than broken fence posts in ensuring that she never stayed tied up and lonely for long, and she completely had my measure when it came to general competence. That day, as so often happened, the saddlebags slipped while I was leading her. And when, as so often happened, I didn't notice and pulled crossly at her rope when she stopped, she looked me straight in the eye with a bored know-all stare, then complacently stood while I grovelled my apologies and tugged at the straps. I had only two weeks to go before I needed to return her and she was doing everything in her power to make me change my mind. Not that I needed any persuasion.

I made my way to Kilworth, a market town with a broad main street, a church, and stone walls shielding Peggy's view of the River Araglin, so we crossed it calmly before turning left towards Lismore. The lane was exceptionally beautiful, winding through deciduous woodland and conifer plantations, with occasional views of the river set in a deeply wooded valley. High hedges shielded large houses and cattle farms – altogether more prosperous-looking than west Cork – with some areas of heathery moorland for additional interest. I crossed the county border into Waterford, and in the early evening rode over the Blackwater River bridge, with its imposing view of Lismore castle, and clip-clopped over the cobblestones of Dervla's courtyard where she and her daughter Rachel were waiting for us.

Chapter 8

August 25th

Dear Kate,

Sorry about the lack of news but there were far more interesting things to do at Dervla's than write letters. But now she and Rachel have gone off to Edinburgh and I've elected to stay on for a few days and house- and pet-sit. It's a responsible job: there are three cats, a flock of bantams, some bantam chicks that'll die in minutes if I don't keep their water filled, and – nicest of all – Orlando, a goat of indeterminate sex, who's suffering from unrequited love for Peggy. He's her host, since she's sharing his orchard, but she's horrid to him, ignoring his adoring eyes and even pretending to bite him. Orlando needs a lot of love. When explaining my duties Rachel said 'sometimes you just have to go out and tell Orlando you love him' and sure enough I sometimes hear him bleating by the gate and go out and stroke him until he's happy. It's lovely being in a house – a real house with a table and a bed and a kitchen and hot water and books and time to enjoy them.

I got a lot of entertainment out of listening to Dervla and Rachel packing for Edinburgh. 'Oh Rachel, that's <u>absurd</u>, you can't take <u>two</u> skirts, says Dervla, packing a briefcase with books. She took no other luggage apart from a small rucksack containing her 'fleabag'. The clothes she was wearing would be perfectly adequate for her appearance as one of the guests of honour at a Literary Event. Just after I'd seen them off I answered the phone and told an elegant-sounding Scottish voice that Dervla was away. "You mean she's left for the airport already?"

"No, she's hitchhiking to Dublin for the ferry."

While the Murphys were here I went riding, blackberrying and mushrooming with Rachel, and now I'm going out for rides on my own to explore the area. Peggy is really enjoying being a normal riding pony without being encumbered with luggage, and gallops and jumps with zest. One day we had a visit from Joe, the ex-tinker who I remember from my last visit when I couldn't understand a word he said. This time I had no problem. He was full of fascinating stories about animals and tinkers. "Know what to do when you see ashes from a tinkers' fire? Dig around and you'll find a horseshoe nail, or maybe a screw... It's the sign of which family was there." He also told me that foxes and badgers are sworn enemies. "A badger can kill a fox easy. Drive them out of the earth by urinating in it. The foxes won't stay then."

And talking of tinkers, Peggy has a mystery in her past. We passed a gypsy camp during one of my rides in the area: an untidy collection of caravans, washing and piebald horses. I thought Peggy would be thrilled by all the horses but she was truly terror-stricken. It took me ages to persuade her to pass, and all the time she made a rather dreadful roaring noise through closed nostrils as though the smell was more than her memory could endure. Strange. Rachel says her pony was equally frightened of them.

I'll end on a pompous note. Last time I was in Lismore I met several people who, when they learned I was here again, have invited me for meals and – this is the good bit – I've dined in a castle two nights running! Different castles, too.

I can't pretend that the Duchess of Devonshire had invited me to dine at Lismore Castle, her Irish home, but the agent was a good friend of Dervla's. At one of these dinners a horsey woman had produced her address book with the assurance that her friends would love to see me and Peggy. Alarmingly, they all lived in houses of sufficient importance to be marked by name on my map. Which was more frightening, I pondered, a Waterford farmer or a 'horse Protestant'? I'd heard a few stories about farmers getting fed up with people camping on their land without permission. "Remember Michael and the Germans? He came across them in his field when he had the front-loader on his tractor. He picked up the tent and dumped them in the ditch while they were sleeping!"

On my last day at Lismore I spread the map on the table and worked out my route via these Big Houses, but left the first part unplanned. I wanted to ride over at least two more mountain ranges before descending to the Tipperary plain. The Knockmealdown Mountains, on Lismore's doorstep, would be the first whichever route I took, but then I had to decide between Galty and Comeragh. They both provided an excuse not to go directly to Limerick where I had to leave Peggy, now horribly close as the crow flies.

U   U   U

Handing over the care of the Murphy animals to a neighbour, I rode out of the yard trying not to listen to Orlando's pitiful bleats as the love of his life clip-clopped away over the cobblestones. Of the two roads over the mountains I chose the one less travelled via the village of Cappoquin. The rain that had fallen during my first couple of days in Lismore had washed the air clean so the Knockmealdown Mountains were purple with heather, not blue with haze. On such a clear day the impressive neo-gothic Mount Melleray monastery, shining grey-white in the foothills against the dark pines, seemed too near to miss. I thought I remembered someone saying

I should visit it, although the only information I could find was that it was built in 1832 by the Cistercians when they were kicked out of Melleray in Brittany. I didn't even know if it was open to the public. Once there, I couldn't find anything to visit except the toilets (and a modern chapel with some good stained glass) but there was some excellent grass and Peggy was hungry so I propped myself against a telegraph pole and had an early lunch. While I was eating, a man strode purposefully towards me. Oh God, was he going to tell me I was trespassing? No, he'd seen the pony and couldn't resist coming over for a chat... What a marvellous way of travelling. He told me Melleray Abbey was famous as a Scout centre: the Scouting headquarters of Ireland, in fact.

The lower flanks of the mountain were covered in conifers, but happily these gave way to heather and gorse as we climbed towards the pass. For the last few days when I'd found myself singing "It's a long way to Tipperary" I'd checked myself and said "It's not actually", so when I reached the county border at the top of the pass and saw 'Tipperary's golden vale' spread out in front of me I felt a real thrill, almost as though Tipperary were my destination. The corn had been harvested and the patchwork fields were not golden but all shades of green and stubble yellow. While I gazed at the view, someone else gazed at me. Why, I wondered, was a sheepdog living here alone, tied to a new and quite cosy-looking kennel? His desirable residence was a good two miles from the nearest house.

The road was unfenced and small sheep tracks ran through the heather in all directions. I couldn't resist attempting a cross-country route down to Newcastle and the River Tar. Peggy was cross at leaving the tarmac. She sulked along, snatching mouthfuls of long grass, but I was ecstatic at this heatherfest. We were waist-deep in purple and mauve bushes buzzing with bees and fluttering with butterflies. The going was rough but dry, and the view open enough that my direction was clear, though I had a few anxieties about the little streams that cut deep channels in the folds of the hills; would the banks be boggy or too steep? And if I did get across would I find a way out at the bottom of the mountains? Although I was now much more confident going across country, I hadn't completely shaken off my fears. Fortunately, sheep paths naturally follow the easiest route and we crossed the streams without difficulty and arrived at a farm track. This led to a gate opening onto a farmyard ankle-deep in slurry. Hysterical dogs barked inside the barns as I nervously made my way out through several more gates on to the road.

The road was little more than a track that, to my delight, turned into a genuine green road (completely covered in grass), running alongside a stream and bordered each side with bracken. I even knew where I was on the map. We emerged in the village of Newcastle and continued east for another few miles before I succumbed to Peggy's increasingly forlorn hints that it was time to stop for the night. My choice of farm was a happy one. The Moores were elderly, outgoing and very friendly. Peggy and the tent went in a large and, considering the drought, miraculously green field with Neddy the donkey, and I accepted the invitation to come to the house for tea. Bread, ham, salad and tomatoes were on offer, along with conversation and a spot of tourism. Mr and Mrs Moore were longing to show me the *lios* in a neighbour's field. After all the myths I'd read about these fairy mounds (or, more mundanely, hillforts) I welcomed the opportunity actually to see one. Archaeologists date them from the Bronze Age, around the 18th century BC. We climbed through a gap in the hedge and saw a symmetrical grass-covered circle surrounded by a depression that may have been a moat. No one knows anything about them, but Mr Moore said someone had excavated the ring and found many small cells; just large enough for a person to squat inside them. There was laughing speculation about small people – fairies. No one believed in them, of course, but when I said I wouldn't mind camping there Mrs Moore said, "Oh dear God, stop! Would you really?"

During our evening chat the Moores said I must visit Vicky, an Englishwoman who had set up as a harness-maker nearby, so after a two-boiled-eggs breakfast I set off for her cottage. She lived alone with no immediate neighbours but dogs, pigs and a mare and foal for company. "A Frenchman who owned this property asked a friend of mine to look after a stallion and some mares for three weeks. He never came back. So I said I'd take a two-year-old filly to break and – poor thing – she was already in foal." Vicky was sitting astride a saddler's bench stitching a browband. Her little workshed was full of tack: racing saddles (Vincent O'Brien commissioned work from her), bridles in for repair, and her favourite, sets of harness in black patent leather. It takes a week to make a saddle, and three weeks for a set of harness.

I left reluctantly and returned to the farm for a second cup of tea and a bottle of milk for the journey. Before going to see Vicky, I'd watched Mrs Moore milk their cow by hand. I envied the practiced ease with which she produced two jets of milk into the pail. I'd once tried this myself, and my aching fingers extracted about a cupful in 15 minutes. "Oh, cows are clever animals. They won't release their milk for someone they don't know. Watch that one, she kicks…"

My next social call – another Moore recommendation – was Pat Melody's bar and trekking centre in Ballymacarbry in the Nire valley. It was always worth talking to stable owners since they knew suitable riding places. Pat and his wife Carmel were as friendly as everyone in this little corner of Waterford. Peggy was given a lunch of horse nuts in the stable while I discussed local trekking over yet more coffee and a sandwich. Pat used to organise a two-day trek in the area but his route was mostly through forestry land and the gates are locked. The usual story.

"I'll open a gate for you," he said. "You can ride for miles in these woods…" and he gave me very specific directions. Then he looked at me speculatively. "You're going to miss the pony when you hand her back, aren't you?" I felt a lump in my throat just thinking about it.

"Would you like to buy her?" A half-formed plan has swept into my head. If Pat bought her, I could see her next time I visited Lismore.

"Sorry," said Pat, "she's too small."

Oh well... Pedar might not want to sell her anyway.

The gate that Pat opened gave me access to a lovely soft pine-needle-covered path that ran for some distance beside an indecisive stream. When I came to a farm and six slavering sheepdogs rushed out, I persuaded myself that Pat didn't actually mean me to go through the farmyard (which, I've since learned, adjoined the road), but to follow the small track that ran behind the buildings. The track meandered aimlessly through the plantations of spruce and pine and it was soon clear that it had no intention of going anywhere near the road. I was furious with myself for once again letting my cowardice contribute to being lost. I kept telling Peggy we'd go on to the next curve, then the next one, so after 45 minutes when I did decide to turn back I was easily tempted to try a path leading off the main track in roughly the right direction.

At least this path took me out into open ground, so I parked Peggy and climbed to a high point to get my bearings. There was no sign of a road, just mountains. Never mind, my compass seemed to think my chosen direction was the right one and my track led to a gate. I decided that if it were open I'd try to make my way across country. Peggy whinnied to me as I returned, but had to resign herself to more cross-country work since the gate was indeed open. The next stretch was moorland, densely covered with heather and sheep, and beyond that was a valley with cultivated fields so presumably with access to a road. I came to a wire mesh fence and followed it around to a place where it had been flattened down either by or for sheep. I covered the mesh with logs and Peggy stepped carefully over into more heather and long grass, with some patches of bog. Peggy pottered along slowly, pretending to look carefully at the ground for a safe foothold (which she was allowed to do) then grab a mouthful of grass (which she was not allowed to do). I saw a farmhouse in the distance and headed with difficulty that way but found, to my disgust, that a deep gully prevented us from reaching it. However, I had more luck with another gap in the fence and soon joined a boreen. To my pleased surprise I was able to follow it safely down the gully, across the river at the bottom, and out onto the road only a few miles above my planned route. Not bad for someone with no sense of direction.

Before long I passed a sign announcing 'Handicrafts, teas, etc.' And thought the 'tea, etc' was too good to miss so tied Peggy up and went inside. I was amazed when the girl looked up from her knitting machine and said, "Oh there you are. We were beginning to think you'd got lost." I was just about to say that she must be mixing me up with someone else when she said that Pat Melody had phoned and asked her to look out for me. He was soon on the scene with the news that he would, after all, like to buy Peggy. I told him I'd contact Pedar as soon as possible.

After tea, Peggy and I headed off into the evening and a pass through the Comeragh Mountains known as The Gap. I was rather excited at doing this – Pat had assured me it should be passable on horseback, though it's shown as a footpath on the map. At least, he said, I would have no problem finding my way since the route is marked with white stakes. It turned out to be one of the loveliest bits of the whole trek and came as an added bonus when I thought I'd finished with good scenery. Peggy and I climbed up through deep heather in full bloom, with the chequerboard fields of Tipperary below and a dramatic gashed and gullied mountain range in subtle greens, greys and heather-mauve to the side. The going was rough. I was considerate and led Peggy who was very tiresome, stopping at intervals and pretending to admire the view and then plunging her head down to snatch mouthfuls to eat. When we got to the top there was no sign of the 'hand of man' in any direction, just mountains, and the going was even more difficult, with some boggy stretches and deep bracken. Then in a V between the hills, there was the vale again, with just a green square lit by the sun like a partly cleaned oil painting.

It was quite late – about 6.30 – and rain clouds were building up behind me, so I decided to look for a suitable campsite. Peggy was telling me that if she didn't have her supper soon she'd die, and I wanted one more night in the wild before heading for civilisation. Soon I came to a flattish area with reasonable grass and a little stream, tethered Peggy to one of the white posts that had so helpfully marked our route, and got the tent set up just before it began to pour. I was worried about Peggy but she turned her back to the wind and waited it out stoically, while I cooked my soup to the pungent smell of burning daddy-longlegs. The heather was infested with them, and they kept flying into the tent and drowning themselves in the wax of my candle.

I woke the next morning to a beautiful sunny day – despite the weather forecast's insistence that it was going to rain – and let Peggy off the tether to fill her stomach further afield. I no longer needed to worry that she'd run away or that I'd be unable to catch her. My plan was to partially circumnavigate Slievenamon, which shows on the map as a brown fingerprint on the green lowlands. It's a strange mountain, an isolated 2,368-foot lump of sandstone with no neighbours. The name means 'Mount of the Women' and features in one of the many legends about Fionn mac Cumhaill (Finn McCool in English) who was Ireland's equivalent of King Arthur. He used to exercise his warriors on the hill (no doubt it muscled them up wonderfully) and when it became time to choose a wife, he thought it would be jolly to sit on top of Slievenamon and award his hand in marriage to the first maiden to reach him. But, sneaky fellow, he'd carried his choice up the mountain the night before, and produced her in triumph just as the first eager sweaty maiden reached the summit. This chosen bride was Gráinne, daughter of Cormac

MacAirt, the High King of Ireland, and she did not share his delight. The legend says that she was repulsed by this man who was the same age as her father, and at her betrothal party fell in love with Diarmuid (Dermot), a man with an irresistible beauty spot, eloped with him and became the stuff of other legends.

Looking at the map it seemed that a half-circuit round the mountain would be feasible in the time available. It would have been had I not taken the wrong turning, and followed several dead-end tracks and tricky cross-country sections before emerging on the right road, but too late to show up at the first Big House where I had an invitation.

Peggy deserved a decent meal so I asked a farmer leaning over a gate if he had a field available. He wasn't sure, but finally decided the clover meadow would be fine and he'd put the old cow elsewhere. "But remember," he said, "clover's very rich. It could make your pony ill." Indeed, I knew that colic could be fatal. For a while I tethered Peggy within reach of some grass, but not the clover, but she looked so anguished at this arrangement that before I went to bed I released her and resigned myself to worrying about her all night. Before I could even get into serious anxiety mode, however, I heard a voice saying "Hello" and there was a woman with a tray piled with sandwiches and biscuits, along with a thermos of tea. "John asked me to look after you," she said. She squatted down outside the tent in the dark, while I rather self-consciously drank the tea and ate the sandwiches, and chatted. She was matron of Kilkenny Orthopaedic Hospital and has nursed in a variety of London hospitals so the conversation centred happily on joint experiences from my previous existence as an occupational therapist.

ʊ ʊ ʊ

It was only six miles to Fethard, a lovely walled town with an ancient church. I felt like Mrs De Winter approaching Mandalay as, in the late morning, I rode up the long stately drive lined with chestnut and oak trees, and passed under two arches to arrive at the splendid 18th-century Grove House. But instead of Mrs Danvers waiting to greet me there was the delightful Rosemary. She was so welcoming to both me and Peggy that I felt perhaps I belonged in a Big House after all. I hadn't really planned to stay, but when I was shown to the spare bedroom I lost the desire to assert myself. Peggy joined some thoroughbreds in a spacious field; I wondered if she'd be ashamed of her working-class origins in such high society.

When Rosemary's husband, Harry, arrived, I soon realised he was one of those rare people, even in Ireland – a brilliant talker. Anecdotes about Irish life just poured out of him and I took to trailing around after him, notebook in hand, trying to record his best stories. "Mikey was helping me make some formal flowerbeds," he told me. "The plan was that I held the string taut so that Mikey could cut the turf in a straight line. This was fine until Rosemary called me into the house for a phone call. I let go of the string and when I returned I found that he had carefully cut round the resulting squiggles." I later met the delightful Mikey who told me that Peggy had "a grand set of legs".

In Ireland the average farm is 60 acres; 20 per cent of farmers own 80 per cent of the land. Grove House had 683 acres. "Yes, it's hard work running such a large farm. Sometimes I think we're crazy." He explained that he wasn't a direct descendant of the original owners but a cousin. And anyway, no one really expected the house to survive the burnings of 1922. The local villagers, however, asked the popular Captain Barton to return. "He should have hung a Union Jack from the window and gone away for a year or so," said Harry ruefully. But there was no concealing how much he loved the estate and had devised all sorts of ingenious ways of managing it.

Describing the economics of rearing bullocks, Harry said, "We're just a warehouse for grass." I'd noticed that each field had a broad solid jump incorporated into the fencing. "We use the horses as bicycles. Cows jump vertically, but horses learn first to jump wide. So we can check on the cattle and get a bit of jumping in at the same time."

Something I was steeling myself to do was phone Pedar to give him a progress report and ask if he might be willing to sell Peggy to Pat Melody. I'd convinced myself that this arrangement would be rather like having a child at boarding school – she might be lonely at first but would soon make friends and I could see her in the holidays. But Pedar said no, he needed her for transport.

It was September 1st. Each day, since Peggy and I had set out on our journey on July 15th, I had measured our mileage on the map with my length of thread and noted the figures in my diary. That night I added them all up and discovered that I had passed the thousand-mile mark.

Chapter 9

As I prepared to leave the next day, Rosemary was bringing horses in, ready for the blacksmith's monthly visit. I'd just finished picking out Peggy's hooves and had noticed how worn her shoes were. Rosemary came over to look, and agreed with me that although she could make it to Limerick with that set, it would be safer – and more considerate to Pedar – to have her re-shod in front. The visiting blacksmith would have no Peggy-sized shoes with him (and wasn't due till the afternoon anyway) but Rosemary gave me his address and phone number. Imagine, a blacksmith with a phone! I had come a long way from the west. In fact, I was noticing all sorts of differences between the prosperous heartlands and the economically depressed regions of Kerry and west Cork. For one thing, there was a greater variety of houses here; instead of the uniform yellow rectangular bungalow or coloured terraced house, there were manors, architect-designed houses and old cottages all mixed together. Earlier, I'd been tickled to pass a cottage with a goat balanced on the windowsill only a mile from a house with a peacock perched on the windowsill.

More prosperity meant more cars, so I took the back roads to my next destination, the Rock of Cashel. This is arguably Ireland's most important religious site and I planned to return and do it properly the next day. I'd already arranged a field with friends of my Lismore contact as well as of Harry and Rosemary. It's a small world, that of the Anglo-Irish. I passed the Rock with its castle magnificently silhouetted against the evening sky and matching the poem I'd copied out from one of Dervla's books.

Royal and Saintly Cashel! I would gaze upon the wreck of thy departed powers.

Not in the dewy light of matin hours,

Nor the meridian pomp of summer's blaze,

But at the close of dim autumnal days,

When the sun's parting glance, through slanting showers,

Sheds o'er thy rock-throned battlements and towers.

Such awful gleams as brighten o'er decay's

Prophetic cheek. At such a time, methinks,

There breathes from thy lone courts and voiceless aisles

A melancholy moral such as sinks

On the lone traveller's heart, amid the piles of vast Persepolis on her mountain stand,

Or Thebes half buried in the desert sand.

(*The Rock of Cashel* by Sir Aubrey de Vere 1788–1846)

The parting glance of the evening sun upon the rock-throned towers exhilarated me, but this lone traveller's heart was struck not by 'melancholy moral' but by Peggy's pleading neigh to stop messing around with a camera and find somewhere for the night.

At the next Big House I was given a luxurious campsite near a spring where the local Girl Guides learn the art of rural survival. Peggy shared a field with Brownie. We felt they'd find a lot to talk about since Brownie too had pulled a trap and travelled around Ireland with a lone adventuress (in this case the au pair) until a broken trace put an end to their journey.

I joined the family for coffee and stories about Tipperary in the old days. My hostess had grown up in the area and remembered the threshing parties in the days before combine harvesters. "Everyone in the village came to help and when it was all done, they feasted on a huge pot of potatoes. There was lots of laughter and merrymaking."

Cashel deserves its tourist rating. So often, a ruin that is impressive from a distance is disappointing when seen at close quarters, or a once-magnificent place is spoiled by tourist gimmicks. Not so the collection of buildings that comprises the Rock of Cashel. The cathedral, chapel and round tower date from the 12th and 13th centuries and had that aura of spirituality that makes you lower your voice, even in a ruin. There is lots to see: Cormac's Chapel, consecrated in 1134, is said to be the finest Romanesque church in Ireland, and there is an abundance of primitive and altogether delightful carvings.

This was the seat of Munster kings from the 4th century to the beginning of the 12th when it was presented to the Church. Indeed, it was said to be the place that St Patrick converted Aengus, the King of Munster, to Christianity. Those medieval stonemasons must have felt close to God as they built their masterpiece so high above the surrounding town. Yet their peasant blood shows in the dumpy Irish Marys portrayed on each side of the cross (you half expect them to be wearing aprons) and the Celtic quality of the stone heads.

I left unsatiated, but aware of Peggy's pleading calls and the need to be at the blacksmith's in time for our afternoon appointment. When I arrived, having trotted much of the way, he was still sweating over the huge hooves of a heavy horse. The owner and I exchanged horse lore while the new shoes were nailed into position, then it was Peggy's turn. She had a newly developed interest in bottoms – I'd had to smack her nose for the nip she'd given me when I mounted that morning – and I just pulled her head up in time as she aimed at Paddy's colourful Y-fronts showing provocatively above his trouser band as he bent over her hoof. He was extraordinarily quick. The old shoes were off and the new ones on in about fifteen minutes. No hot-shoeing here.

ʊ   ʊ   ʊ

My next hosts lived five miles away. They were expecting me so I was only slightly surprised to be greeted by a red-haired man and two boys who emerged from the woods some distance from the house. They were searching for some missing calves, they told me. My arrival must have been hideously inconvenient; the previous day they had been host to the riding part of a tetrathlon and on the following day two of the five children were returning to boarding school. This was Ireland, however, and here was another deeply religious, warm, entertaining and relaxed family who effortlessly incorporated my new face at the dinner table.

Two more new faces turned up while we were eating: a rather formidable French couple who were doing something with horses in the next valley. On being introduced, the woman lowered herself down next to me like an eagle landing on its eyrie, twisted sideway so she could stare into my face and said:

"How old are you?"

"Forty-three."

"*Mais non*, that is not true!"

"Yes, it is."

"No!"

"All right then, I'm twenty-six."

"No!"

Fortunately her husband then called her away; I had a nasty feeling she expected me to say 60 so she could talk about grandchildren.

I was summoned to breakfast next morning by one of the boys driving a 1950s' tractor. Though only 15 he had a passionate interest in fixing up antique vehicles and was a dab hand at welding. I was back in mushroom country so breakfast was one of those marvellous black-stained fry-ups with lots of brown bread. I left with my saddlebags bulging with a picnic lunch and instructions for my final diversion through the Glen of Aherlow and into the Galty Mountains. I'd first heard about the Galtys from the man who chatted to me at the Mt Melleray monastery. He thought it the loveliest place in Ireland (so did Arthur Young, writing 200 years ago: 'Those who are fond of scenes in which nature reigns in all her wild magnificence, should visit this stupendous chain').

The old Celtic gods and heroes were busy around here and the largest of the corrie lakes, which are a feature of the Galtys, is said to have been formed when the ground opened up under the spell of harp-playing Cliach who was trying to win the heart of Princess Baina, daughter of the king of the fairies. Despite his sitting on top of the mountain for a year, working on two harps simultaneously, she never succumbed to his charms so the earth received him into its bosom. Or possibly into fairyland. Or maybe they're the same thing. Hard to tell, sometimes.

It was to Lough Muskry that I set off rather reluctantly on the grey morning of September 2nd. The weather was unpromising for a mountain excursion and I was suffering from that mixture of depression and anticipation that, for me, marks the end of a trip. Part of me was looking forward to going home and part of me dreaded parting with Peggy whose daily demonstrations of affection – or dependency – made it even harder. But the part that hated leaving Ireland told me I'd regret not seeing as much of the Galty Mountains as possible, so I took the sign-posted track through the conifers, opened a gate, and followed a good path to a stream. The view was pleasant and, in sun, would probably have been inspiring. But I was spoiled; I'd seen too many superlative mountain scenes and a river and some brown-green hills under a chill sky were not good enough. I sat by the stream, ate my ham sandwiches, and let the cloud of melancholy settle over me.

"Excuse me. Is it safe to pass your pony?" The English couple had come down from the lake. I asked them about the trail. "I don't think the pony will make it up there, it's a bit of a scramble." Having come so far I thought I ought to have a look, so I unbagged and unsaddled Peggy and tethered her for a prolonged lunch hour. As I climbed up in drizzle through the coarse grass I saw a rather large horse grazing further up the mountain not far from Peggy. Suppose it heard Peggy – it would be just like her to give an experimental neigh – and galloped over and broke its legs on the tether chain? Suppose it was a stallion and tried to have its wicked way with her? Climb, climb, worry, worry. It was further than I expected (it always is) to the ridge, but worth the effort. Sheep scattered as the lake came suddenly into view. A black, grim lough scooped out by glaciers below the wet, grim brown-grey cliffs. In sun, it's probably a blue lake under golden sandstone. I rather liked it grim.

The two horses were still unacquainted when I got back to the stream. We jogged briskly down through the woods, with Peggy nurturing her little victory of not having climbed to the lake, and headed west along the road. A car full of giggling nuns drew up.

"Have you heard the results?"

"What?"

"Now how would she be hearing the results?"

They all collapsed in delighted laughter. "Hurling. It's the big match. You didn't know?"

∪ ∪ ∪

I was heading for Ballinacourty House. The estate once owned much of the Glen of Aherlow, then, under the Land Reform Acts, most of the acreage was handed over to the tenants and finally in 1922 the Big House was burned. All that remains are the stables which were occupied by Eamon De Valera and his troops during the civil war. They had been converted into a rather posh bed-and-breakfast place with the grounds serving as a camp and caravan park. I'd been told about Ballinacourty by a couple of people, so it was an obvious choice for that night. Besides, Peggy had become such a snob she automatically turned into Big House drives.

Jennie La Haye was quietly amused by my request. She called her husband and said, "This visitor wants bed and breakfast." He looked at me, unimpressed. "Go on, look outside." Peggy and Peter had different ideas of what constitutes luxury horse accommodation. I knew Peggy would prefer a field, Peter was sure a well-appointed stable was everything her equine heart could desire. There was no field anyway, so Peggy was led to a Stately Stable where she contrived to look as pathetic as possible, propping her nose on the high door, whinnying to be let out, and refusing at first to eat the considerately provided hay and horse nuts. She was by now such a mistress of manipulation that I spent the evening (reserved for finishing my book) trailing up and down the drive so she could eat grass, answering questions from a gaggle of children, and lifting them onto her bare back.

I was half woken in the early morning by a blackbird singing a very sweet, very leisurely solo from a branch immediately above the tent. Then, as the chatter and clamour and tantalising bacon smells from the other campers began to permeate my world, I reached for my cup and saucepan and started boiling the water for tea.

Peggy was touchingly pleased to see me. I could see from the particles of sawdust sticking to her sides that she did at least lie down during the night so couldn't have been too miserable. I led her into the campground and, under the eyes of a dozen or so campers, groomed her, saddled up, bagged up and set off towards my final bit of sightseeing: Lough Gur. This lake and its surroundings were described in my guidebook as having 'a remarkable number of Stone Age dwellings and burial places' and I'd been urged by Pat Melody to see it. It was also on the way to Boher, where I had to leave Peggy for Pedar to collect. The morning was cloudy and blustery with rain promised by the Met man. At least, for once, I was prepared, with all my waterproof gear in an accessible place in the saddlebag. The first drops fell shortly after I'd left the campground, and soon Peggy was as black and slippery as a sea lion, but without its cheerfulness. She plodded along with her head down and sideways and ears back. I hunched myself in my anorak and felt the rain gradually trickle into my boots via my socks. I'd had a choice: rain trousers which kept my bottom dry and feet wet (because they're too short) or rain chaps which allowed me dryish feet but a clammy wet bottom. I'd chosen the former. Shortly after noon, I passed a lone pub. It was called the Welcome Inn. On the side was painted in bold black letters 'You are welcome in'. We plodded by. After a hundred yards I turned Peggy round towards the welcome. What the hell, it was nearly lunchtime and a Guinness under cover would be much nicer than marmite sandwiches and water on a rain-soaked saddle-table. I tied Peggy to a telegraph pole and went inside. The bar was empty. I stood and dripped onto the multi-coloured carpet until an elderly woman sidled in and looked at me suspiciously.

"I'd like a drink, please," I said cheerily. Silence. She regarded me balefully.

"What sort of drink?"

"Oh, a Guinness will do nicely. A bit wet isn't it? But I suppose we mustn't complain, the farmers will be happy." I burbled on.

"You on a bicycle or something?"

"No, a horse."

"Well, for God's sake!" She padded to the door and looked at Peggy then disappeared into the public bar to haul out the only other customer for a view. The atmosphere warmed, conversation began, and soon a complimentary plate of sandwiches had joined my Guinness. The other customer, a very portly man, was evidently a semi-professional pubber. He had a small stock of jokes which he produced and which I laughed at, I hoped in the right places since I didn't understand them.

The conversation moved on to witchcraft and Biddy Early. "You don't know who she is? They called her the Witch of Clare. She could talk to the *sidhe*. You know, the fairies." His grandfather remembered her; she died in 1874. "Oh yes, she could cast spells all right. But she cured people as well, mind you." Apparently Biddy had a great way with herbs and was as successful with animals as humans. The talk turned to a local woman who had a cure for shingles. Ears pricked for some gem of folk medicine, I asked what exactly she did. "Oh, she gives them a few sips of 7-Up and says something."

Before I could ask him to elaborate, I heard a neigh. Reluctantly, I peeped out of the door at Peggy's back view but she seemed all right so I returned to the bar. Another louder, longer neigh. Peggy's head was turned towards the pub entrance as far as her short rope would allow, and she was demanding my return. Overcome, as usual, by remorse at my boozy ways, I asked for a bucket of water and a piece of bread, paid for my drink and left.

At least the rain had stopped and we continued through pleasant scenery towards Lough Gur. I pulled out my book from the saddlebag and read the last couple of chapters, letting Peggy find her own way and return the astonished stares of passing cyclists.

Since we'd made an early start I told Peggy she could stop at 6. I selected a freshly painted yellow farmhouse set inside a frame of green fields with a long gravel driveway. My toes curled with anxiety as a group of Alsatians and Dobermans leapt up at my approach, followed by a large unfriendly-looking man. I put the usual question. "I wouldn't say we had." I smiled sweetly, thanked him, and turned the reluctant Peggy round. The next farmhouse was by the road and not as smart. There was no reply when I knocked on the door.

Peggy neighed, and I could hear a shuffling and key clanking and a "Who is it?" Always a hard question to answer, but the door was cautiously opened. An elderly woman wearing one purple stocking listened to my request. "I don't think so, but I'm not the boss." She directed me to the farmyard where an old man emerged from the cowshed at the same time as his purple-stockinged wife came out of the back door. While waiting for their son, the boss, to arrive they looked me over appraisingly.

"Are you on your own?"

"Yes."

"Single?"

"Yes."

"Do you want to get married?"

"Well, not tonight."

The good-looking son appeared and said, "'Tis no problem. Which field would you like?" He suggested a paddock, three gates further down the road, almost overlooking Lough Gur, and with piped water for Peggy and me. He also gave me some milk and offered his phone so I could let Mr O'Connell know that I would be delivering Peggy tomorrow.

It was a pleasant paddock with some excitable cattle bellowing from a neighbouring field and high hedges providing protection from the wind. The grey cloud had rolled away leaving the usual Irish green-blue evening sky. This would be my last night camping with Peggy and I sat outside the tent watching her before I prepared my evening meal, pinning a picture in my memory. I'd told Pedar that I would bring her back a better pony, and I was right. Her Guinness-coloured coat shone in the evening sun, her sides were plump, her quarters well-rounded and she looked superbly fit. Which she was. Her regime for the last seven weeks had been almost identical to the conditioning exercise given to young race horses; hours of walking and slow trotting. Although a daily feed of oats might have given her more pep, she had obviously thrived on her diet of grass which had almost always been green and succulent despite the drought. And what luck I'd had with the weather! The downpour today – only a few hours in fact – served as a reminder of how little rain I'd had. I'd never been drenched to the skin, and in the whole 2 ½ months of the journey there had been only about five wet days. And this in the west of Ireland, one of the wettest regions in Europe. As one old Irishman put it, it had been 'the driest summer that came since the history of time!'.

                            ∪   ∪   ∪

My plan for the last day was to arrive in Boher around noon and hope to get a lift into Limerick so I could catch the evening train to Dublin, but my subconscious had its delaying tactics and it was nearly 6 o'clock before I turned into Ted O'Connell's farm. I had found Lough Gur more interesting than expected.

The first archaeological site I'd come to was 'The Giant's Grave'. This was marked on my map and looked worth the short diversion. If a giant is buried there he must have been in two sections since the grave has two chambers. In fact it's a 'wedge-shaped gallery grave' which was the prehistoric (around 2000BC) resting-place for eight adults and four children. It was not hard to believe that a giant was involved in the construction of it, though. The sides were composed of a double wall of stone slabs with five massive stones resting on top, one of which is reckoned to weigh fifty tons or more. The grave overlooked the lake which must have been of special significance to the Bronze-Age Irishmen. They built their rectangular and circular houses around the shore, a *crannog* (small defended artificial island) in the lough, and also an impressive stone circle like a junior Stonehenge and roughly the same age, keyed to the summer solstice.

Lough Gur was a settlement as far back as 3000BC and the stone circle was built by the 'beaker folk' at the beginning of the Bronze Age. That metal, an alloy of copper and tin, was worked in Ireland between about 2000BC and 300BC when it was replaced by iron. One particularly fine piece of bronze workmanship was found here. Known as the Lough Gur shield it was discovered in 1872 in the marshy fringes of the lake, and sold for 30 shillings. There's a copy of this circular shield in the visitors' centre which was my next stop. Thought to date from 700BC, it's decorated with raised rings and bumps which, the label explains, reduced the impact of a sword. An undecorated bronze disc thick enough to withstand a slash from a sword would have been too heavy. The original Lough Gur shield is in the National Museum in Dublin, along with a mind-boggling display of gold artefacts dating from the same period. After visiting Lough Gur and following it up with a trip to the museum in Dublin, no-one could call the Irish a backward nation. Irish accomplishments in craftsmanship nearly 3,000 years ago surpass those of Britain. How much had we set these creative people back by colonisation and oppression, I wondered?

I spent quite a time at the visitors' centre knowing that Peggy was happily tethered on the picnic site, cropping the short but very sweet grass. I also wryly noticed that although she'd given one of her affectionate whinnies when I'd returned from the Giant's Grave, I only merited a sour look when I interrupted her lunch to continue our journey. I'd had my own midday meal with Desmond and his wife Mary, after he'd stopped his car to talk to me, happily accepting his invitation for tea at their house just down the road. He was an interesting man, having been a National Hunt jockey, a stunt rider in Hollywood, a long-distance lorry driver, and a breeder of mountain lions (pumas), of all things. He was now trying to get permission to set up a wildlife park in the grounds of a stately home that had recently been bought by Arabs.

By the time I rode away from Lough Gur it was mid afternoon. I sat on Peggy with my aching bottom and an aching heart. I looked at her sweet little ears, sharply pricked with their foamy markings around the base, and thought how empty the view of future lanes would seem without this familiar foreground. I also realised that she no longer carried herself like a carthorse. Her head was now high and her neck arched. Pretty as a picture, she was.

According to my map, Boher was just across the main road and over a railway line. Sure enough, I soon came to a church and the scatter of houses that I'd been told was the centre of town. Someone directed me to the O'Connells. I'd expected a crumbling run-down farmhouse and was impressed – and intimidated – by the long drive leading to a large white house. It looked deserted. I tied Peggy to a tree where, to her disgust, she couldn't eat, so added her neighs to my timid knocks. As I expected, there was no answer so I led Peggy back to a grassy area to graze while I made some further investigations. Then I realised that only the front of the house looked deserted. Around the back I found cars and an open door. A girl was cooking dinner in the kitchen. I explained who I was and a young man appeared to show me where I could put Peggy for the night. He told me I could pitch my tent on the lawn outside the house.

"But I want to sleep in the field with the pony," I said, struggling to keep my voice steady, "it's our last night together."

"Well, I suppose it'll be all right," he said, as we led her through gooey cow dung in the farmyard and into a paddock already occupied by an inquisitive piebald gelding.

While I was unloading the bags, father Ted appeared on the scene and questioned why I was not pitching my tent on the lawn.

"She wants to sleep with the pony" said the son, rolling his eyes. Ted thought this plan absurdly sentimental. Out of the question, in fact.

"You can sleep in the house or in your tent near the house, and you can visit the pony at hourly intervals throughout the night if you want."

Watching Peggy and the piebald having a kicking match, I agreed that maybe it would be more sensible to camp on the lawn after all, so together we heaved the luggage back.

I was invited in for tea and stayed to help peel – and eat – six buckets of mushrooms. I'd seen no mushrooms since my bonanza in west Cork but Co Limerick seemed to be carpeted with them. My eyes and fingers itched to do some picking, so I was pleased when Sean, one of the sons, said that I could collect my own the next morning. They'd make a nice present for my friend Dorothy, who I would stay with in Dublin before catching the ferry back to Holyhead. "Go to the third field over there," he said pointing, "and you'll be tripping over them."

I got up early next morning and packed up for the trip home. The saddle had to be stripped of its girth and stirrups and put in a bag, and a handle devised so I could carry it. I sorted through the saddlebags, throwing out all my 'keep in case I need them' bits and pieces and giving useful heavy things like the tether chain ("Lovely, that'll be just right for the bull") to the farmer and tied the bags up into a bundle with the reins. Then I picked up the plastic water-bucket and headed for the fields for my final fungus foray.

I thought I'd understood where the good mushroom field was, but each meadow I walked across was a smooth expanse of green with not a white blob in sight. Or they were full of thistles and rushes, or calves which latched onto this promising-looking woman carrying a bucket, with enthusiasm. There didn't seem to be many gates and I had to scramble through barbed-wire fences, or slide down muddy banks into water-filled ditches then haul myself up the other side. I began to regret my mushroom greed and looked anxiously at my watch. I'd been offered a lift into Limerick "sometime in the morning" and didn't think it polite or expedient to be gone for too long. I'd set out before 8 and it was already nearly 9 o'clock. Then I saw them. A green field so densely dotted with white it looked like a spotted tablecloth. I was indeed tripping over mushrooms. After a few minutes I became so selective I was only picking perfect white domes with pink gills and ignoring the older or slug-nibbled specimens. It didn't take long to fill the bucket and start back towards the farm which was, after all, only three fields away. But the hedges were high and I couldn't actually see the house. I crossed several fields, none of which seemed to have a gate. One meadow had a very large, very menacing bull in it; I sidled round the edge wondering if bright-yellow plastic is as inflammatory to a bull as a red cape. Finally, to my great relief, I saw the farm buildings, with a nice boreen leading to them. When I arrived in the farmyard, however, I realised things weren't quite right. "Oh God, this isn't the right farm," I thought, as a small dog rushed out from behind a wall with its tail between its legs, followed by a flying wellington boot. Then came the farmer's wife who didn't seem in the least put out to discover a guilt-ridden English woman clutching a bucket of mushrooms in her farmyard. "Oh my, you have got a lot!" she said pleasantly as I muttered my apologies for trespassing. "You want the O'Connells? It's not far, just a couple of houses that way. You can't miss it."

I walked up the long drive towards the road and wondered where the hell I was. The road didn't look familiar and a few tentative steps in the direction she'd indicated confirmed my suspicions that it was the wrong O'Connell. I started jogging in the direction I felt was right, then realised the stupidity of relying on my 'sense of direction' and knocked at the door of a bungalow. It was opened immediately by a fat, greasy but very friendly old man who'd obviously been watching my progress through lace curtains since he directed me "the way you were going, but it's quite a way." He added, "Well over a mile." I looked at my watch. I'd already been gone two hours. "Typical!"

I thought to myself sourly, "I go over a thousand miles without getting seriously lost, and look how I finish." Switching the mushroom bucket to my less aching left hand I set off down the road.

All that was left now was to say goodbye to Peggy. I could procrastinate no longer. When I arrived at her field she threw up her head, whinnied and walked towards me with pricked ears. Her piebald friend then trotted up for his share of the titbits. Peggy wasn't having this and ran at him with ears flattened and teeth bared. He turned round to kick her, she squealed, and my oft-rehearsed goodbye scene dissolved into equine squabbles. I couldn't hug her, I couldn't give her a kiss on the nose, I couldn't even stroke her. I just said, "Goodbye, Peggy. And thank you," and walked away, wiping the tears from my cheeks.

U U U

The Dublin taxi driver who took me to the coach station was talkative. What had I been doing in Ireland, he wanted to know, and how long had I been here? I told him, trying to keep the pride out of my voice and to assume tones of appropriate modesty. "You came over just to ride a horse around?" he asked incredulously, "No other reason?"

Epilogue

That was it. I never saw Peggy again, nor tried to keep in touch with Pedar. I didn't want the heartache of failure. And I knew she would be all right. After a holiday in Boher she would be taken back to Dingle and resume her job pulling Pedar's gig. She would sleep in the same field each night, with the same horse companions. And that would be enough; horses, like all animals, need routine to keep them happy.

I had taken Peggy out of her comfort zone and she had responded heroically. In the place of other horses she had bonded with me, as I had with her. But it's taken 30 years of hindsight to appreciate just how much I owe her.

When I started the trek, with Mollie, I was still in the mindset that the most important part of horse management was control. Was the pony obedient? Could I make it do what I wanted? By the end of the journey I had learned that it was as important for me to understand what the pony was trying to tell me, as it was to impose my will on the animal. Peggy was the catalyst in that transition. As I'd remarked when I first had her, I'd never known such an extrovert, sociable horse. Communication was her thing, so communicating with me came naturally. I am ashamed, now, at how slow I was to learn that any strange behaviour was her attempt to tell me something, rather than sheer naughtiness.

Horses are perhaps unique in our animal-doting world. We love them, we try to bond with them, and then we sell them on. A talented horse will have several owners during its 30-year lifetime, and goodness knows how many riders. Each time it changes hands it is expected to make the adjustment and respond with generosity. Most horses do. That is an extraordinary and deeply touching fact.

My thousand miles through Ireland changed me forever. I learned how to cope alone with triumph and disaster, how to enjoy my solitary state and to live in the present as time slipped by. I learned about generosity, about the old, old human attribute of hospitality to strangers. I learned about the history of Ireland and the uncomfortable fact of my country's oppression, and I learned that this is one of the most beautiful places in Europe. But, above all, I treasure that opportunity to get to know, and be friends with, Mollie and Peggy.